Towards the Equator

By the same author:

Poetry
The Rearrangement (1988)
Sleeve Notes (1992)
Infinite City (1999)
The Man and the Map (2003)
Autographs (2008)

The Attic (2013)
(bilingual: trans. Jacques Rancourt)

Fiction
The Poet (2005)

Towards the Equator
New & Selected Poems

Alex Skovron

PUNCHER & WATTMANN

© Alex Skovron 2014

This book is copyright. Apart from any fair dealing for the purposes of study and research, criticism, review or as otherwise permitted under the Copyright Act, no part may be reproduced by any process without written permission. Inquiries should be made to the publisher.

First published in 2014. Reprinted in 2015, 2016, 2017, 2024.
Published by Puncher & Wattmann
PO Box 279
Waratah NSW 2298

http://www.puncherandwattmann.com
web@puncherandwattmann.com

A catalogue record for this book is available from the National Library of Australia

Skovron, Alex
Towards the Equator: New & Selected Poems
ISBN   9781922186553

Cover design by David Musgrave
Edited by David Musgrave
Text in Adobe Garamond Pro 11/14.8
Printed by McPherson's Printing Group

This project has been assisted by the Australian Government through the Australia Council, its arts funding and advisory body.

for Mietek Skovron
(1912–2013)

Contents

Towards the Equator: New Poems

Four Nights	3
History	4
Possible Friends	5
A Cup of Tea	7
Imperium	8
The Needle	9
The Belltower	10
Next Day the Weather	11
Collision	12
Humility	13
Precious Cargoes	14
Boy	16
The Secret	18
Riveder le Stelle	20
The Attic	21
Sanctum	22
Kandukur	23
Waking on the Last Morning of the Twentieth Century	24
Indefinite Articles	25
Malvern Interlude	26
Her Century	27
Sin Tacks	28
Confutatis	29
Jam	31
Quest	32
De la Nature	33
My Wattle Princess	34
Ark	36
Once We Crossed the Equator	38
The Sky-Tree	40
Full Moon, Thebes	41
Denizen	42

Semper Fidelis	43
Microcosmos	44
The Steeples	46
She	47
What the Dead Do	49
The Last Word	50

from *The Rearrangement* (1988)

A Concise History of the Moon	53
Cyril and the Snails	59
The Composer on his Birthday	60
A Song at Last	61
An Intelligent Conversation	62
Into the Heart Again	64
Wondernight	65
Springvale	68
Elsternwick	69
Optical Illusions	70
Lines from the Horizon	74
Sentences	84
From an Interview with a Faded Juggler	86
Election Eve, with Cat	88
Fugue	89
The Rearrangement	95
A Girl of Nagasaki	103
The Death of the Word	104
Narrowing of the Arteries	105
Arrival	106

from *Sleeve Notes* (1992)

Sisyphus	111
What Matters	112
The Old Song	113
German China	114
On the Theology of Ants	116
After a Meeting of the Mahler Society, Melbourne, 1952	118

Quadrilateral	119
A Lecture in the Public Library	127
The Face in the Flower	128
Also Silence	130
The Golden Age	133
Ambit	134
Fragment	135
Elgar Revisits Worcestershire, 1984	137
A Life	138
Sleeve Notes	141
The Waterline Poems	152
Beyond Nietzsche	160

from *Infinite City* (1999)

House	165
Memento Mori	165
Don Giovanni's Prayer	166
Time	166
Chess	167
The Castle	167
Linkage	168
The Infinite City	168
Cabaret	169
The Desk-chair	169
The Jester	170
Art	170
Faking It	171
Extended Cadences	171
Mona Lisa	172
Oasis	172
Galatea	173
The Date	173
Histories	174
The Journey	174
Vespers	175
The Hair	175

Safe Purchase	176
Liberian Seaman	176
The Note	177
Winding Up	177
Narcissus	178
Office Party	178
Water Music	179
Homo Singularis	179
Outrageous Fortune	180
Bless Relaxes	180
Lullabies	181
Flash Pan	181
Historian	182
Syzygy	182
Meeting of Minds	183
Imperfect Rhymes	183
Smoke '62	184
They Sing	184
The New World	185
The Keys	185
Chalkmarks	186
Against the Grain	186
Glissando	187
Sunspots	187
Millennium	188
Umbrage	188
Night Journeys	189
For Light	189
Like Music	190
Omen	190
The Golem	191
Distorting Venice	191
Untergang	192
After Messiaen	192
Credo	193

from *The Man and the Map* (2003)

from Polish Corridors	197
Retracing the Map	200
Observatorium	202
The Wooden Box	203
Passive Smoking	204
Legend	206
Quicksilver	208
Ago	209
Eclipse	212
It	214
Washington Pilgrim	215
Mr Wilkinson	216
Elegy	220
The Violin-maker, the Forest and the Clock	222
from Vienna	229
After the Future	234
The Guilt Factory	236
Turning the Tableland	238
The Centuries	241
On the Road to Hell	242
The Man and the Map	245
Palace Coup	248
A Marriage	250
The Ferris Wheel	251
Some Precepts of Postmodern Mourning	255
Supper Song	257
Dreams of Dead Poets	258

from *Autographs* (2008)

Possession	263
Supplication	264
Mirror	265
Amphora	266
Bite	267
Ladies	268

Dance	269
Mood	270
Home	271
Surrender	272
Encounters	273
Village	274
Projections	275
Room	276
Lustspiel	277
Radius	278
Dysphoria	279
The	280
Haftarah	281
Mission	282
Verberations	283
Dialectic	284
Conclave	285
Threshold	286
Signs	287
Shadow	288
Notes	290
Acknowledgments	292

Towards the Equator

New Poems

Four Nights

Somewhere a dog barks,
    the shock of splintered glass,
    a muffled scream, then
    the Adriatic silence.

A child somewhere, wading a rectangle
    of corn in the mosaic dark,
    searchlights ripple methodically
    the frown of a pond.

Two trains cross each other somewhere,
    a razor line walks the ceiling,
    crockery trembles
    tactfully, a horse-drawn wagon
    two villages away, clumsy
    on the road to Kostolac.

Somewhere nothing changes,
    except two clouds have parted
    to grant the craning moon
    a glimpse into a first-floor window,
    where a woman leans out,
    scans the corner again, resigned
    to the costumed mob
    that any minute must appear.

History

'But the past was there, waiting for him, watching him.'
— Milan Kundera, *Ignorance*

On the sidewalks of the city I've discovered
the walking numberless, a myriad gliding heads,
from each of which (an airship suspended above it)
there trails a bubble by the flimsiest of threads.
Its envelope might be cloudlike, wavelike, round,
or cleanly rectilinear; every balloon contains
a moving picture, a fragment denoting sound,
or a sentence scrolling forward. It maintains
its floating fixity atop each hurrying figure
(bobbing a little in momentum's drag) –
yet when I frown to make sense of the design,
it shimmers from my gaze, or something bigger
on the street distracts …
                    No one can translate another's flag:
I can scarcely, in the mirror, decipher mine.

Possible Friends
(after Adam Zagajewski)

Those who no longer exist
are the ones, bittersweet, we cling to.

Their keepsakes we embrace
too late: his capricious tartan scarf

you never wore, her booklet
of psalms and proverbs – they sting us

from what might have been, brittle
channels in the brickwork

of lost choices. And then
the universe of strangers, so-described:

that Heathrow cabbie
you converted to an ancient cousin

and then tipped profusely
as a kind of penance, the old Belgrade poet

who pocketed, 'for *you*',
a two-millennium tile at Viminacium

(you tried so hard yet he couldn't grasp
your refusal, your antique ethics),

or the aging waitress at LAX
diminished over a perfect spoilt romance,

her voice a far-off waltz
you almost recognized from – where?

How many faces in the pinball metropolis
with proud eyes flashing by

are faces we have once crossed already
(and if not, in a previous life);

how many, in a parallel moment,
if we should only stop each other to listen,

might grow into our lifelong familiars –
to sit with us, debate Heraclitus,

elucidate the essence of the Preludes,
or tell us just who we are?

A Cup of Tea

When he tries to recall the details, his mind goes blank.
After all, so many years have passed; and after all,
it was simply a moment's impulse, a chancy fling.

She was battling an inverted umbrella, her clothes a mess,
two bulky carrybags dumped in the slicing wind;
so he'd stopped the car, tooted, beckoned her over.

This was a time when you still could trust a stranger,
people accepted lifts, and people gave. Especially in weather
like this. She tumbled in.

Her Levis were soaked to black, t-shirt translucent,
hair a cascade, her lips a despairing smile; but in the eyes
he glimpsed an ingenuous calm.

So he ferried her home – a hefty drive, the grimmer side of town;
but he'd insisted, and her protests were undisguised.
Of course she invited him in, a cup of tea for his trouble.

She sat him down, went off to remove the wet, returned
in this terry-towel thing, a kind of jumpsuit with a luscious scent,
and suddenly they were coiled on the floral couch.

That's where the particulars grow dim,
though he remembers a gloomy pendulum ticking, a TV chatting
uselessly, the salt taste of her tongue.

The rest is vague, except for the way she cried,
and clung, and pressed him into her skin, as if to whisper
some atrocious cliché, like 'I'll never let you go …'

Now here she is, so altered, so many years.
But there's something about the tall companion beside her,
the half-familiar mirror of his gaze.

Imperium

Memory takes us for a ride, and we it –
Time clocks its vengeance on forgetfulness;
When the god Remembrance comes calling
(Old Eros in a mask) we repossess

In vain the confabulated latitudes
For our retelling, now tainted and digital;
Far below the long-relinquished Equator
Our analog histories in the original

Lie in dust like Alexandrian manuscripts
Or sunk, an irretrievable Atlantis;
So we puzzle over what preceded Genesis
As we wait for Revelation to supplant us.

And so history is our cross and our salvation,
We genuflect before its stations, cosily;
From the first sad Romulus to the last
A hundred dozen winters weave a rosary

We can say in one chart or chapter,
And we joy ourselves then, or else we cry;
And we fix memory's shingle to our future –
We will miss ourselves when we die.

The Needle

It was a day between the wars
      like any other, a calligraphy of trucks
      and taxis, carts and trolley-buses,
      fresh rain swirling the glossy boulevards,
      umbrellas erupting like inkblots
      in the electric mist, chaos of a cloudbreak
      awakened on a sluggish afternoon.

We clung to the café window
      near the corner of Schelling and Duclos
      counting, for there was little to be gained in talk,
      the uniforms and their lapel graffiti
      that glowed like Rothkos in the thunder-light
      as the avenue slowly drowned in dark.

Not just raindark or fading dusk:
      it seemed the very – what? – the sky itself,
      if not about to drag the curtain
      down on accustomed certainties, at least
      glowered (ah yes!), with a laconic knowledge,
      an inaudible rumble that I swore

Must come from deep in the earth –
      a bass undergrounding the Fauré quartet
      our porcelain waitress had threaded
      to the gramophone hidden under the counter,
      and I listened with the expectancy
      of a seismologist hunched over a graph
      for the delicate needle to jump.

The Belltower

We had been walking about
>in the torrid air, our elbows nudging
>and an unspoken pact, humid and delicious,
>had arisen in the shrinking spaces
>between us. You went so far

As to hint a continuance
>on the morrow, and I exulted in the strangest
>comfort I'd permitted myself
>since the start of the war. So we strolled
>on among the dusty pigeons

That swept and reswept
>each minute the cobblestones of the piazza,
>and without speaking we turned as one
>toward the tiny curtained café
>in the corner under the belltower

Just as the clock struck
>one. You trembled then, I don't know why,
>but the note was shocking, peremptory,
>and we looked into each other
>as if for the first time

Then lowered our eyes clumsily,
>and that was when you took my hand
>for the first time and stopped,
>so I stopped too. And we stood there like that,
>under the bell and the glib sky.

Next Day the Weather

The next day the weather changes.
Clouds the shade of ash and honey stretch
the strings of the sky, are echoed
in purple chords of thunder. A gusty rain
lashes the mushroom chimneys,
the satellite dishes. Our room high above
the Avenue of the Commemorations
trembles after each sizzled flash
traces its nervous network on the ceiling
of our thoughts. You laugh,
you weep. I pace the corral of an open page
that refuses to turn, the words swirl
their tumbleweed before my eyes. Who
can tell, and why? Somewhere in this city
a poet splices the penultimate line
into the masterpiece he will never write,
a magician behind a Steinway is shaking
the universe from his sleeve,
down in the street a garbled figure
stumbles into a rain-hatched archway,
a stray hound examines the air;
and you, outstaring the window, waiting
for doubt and the downpour to settle in.

Collision

'… it is my ambition always to know more
than the surface discloses.'
— Stefan Zweig

He watches colonnades of cars from the twentieth floor
Crawl onto the Bridge, sips a double Dimple,
Perusing his city. Can't let go the accident he saw
Next to the Park, a hatchback and a truck, a simple
Prang – the Colt tried to cut in, nobody hurt;
But it's the moment's unique perfection he can't forget,
Its sheer lovely necessity – yes, that's the word,
The somehow utter *need* for their collision. Yet
That's not quite it either. Was it how unbendingly
Both drivers disembarked, or how the truckie,
Regulation muscle and tattoo, shook his head slowly,
Gazing at the girl, his mouth maybe chiding how lucky
She'd been – while she, her hair unbundled
By a new gust, began to weep, and as he reached to pat
Her shoulder to console, she seemed to crumple
Into his sheltering bulk, and there they stood, like that,
Holding each other while the traffic tumbled,
A knot islanded amid the flow of the city's sap …
And as he sips, a photo collides with his eye:
A face framed on the desktop watches her father cry.

Humility

For months Mozart has been so crucial I haven't played him.
The winds, filibustering the house, have heard
the chimney crackle and the paint strain
while the old obsessions went ignored. What was the point?
One evening I flipped the LP of the A major (K.488)
and the slow movement lacerated my defences
all over again. I squinted beyond the buddleia
on the fenceline and thought I could discern vast citadels
circling the horizon, and it was almost a joy
that swept its andante through the sad molecules
of my imaginings – but just then
a magpie alighted on the lawn, dragging a shadow
behind it as the sky turned a molten gold and a storm
broke from the west. The disc had ended
(I had no recollection of having heard the rondo finale)
and I sprang to the phone, jangling churlishly
to tell me you were gone. Music is like that:
it knows. It brought to mind what you had shown me
on the Baltic coast under the lighthouse:
twirling a miniature sailboat of souvenir amber
between thumb and forefinger, you pointed to the tower
and the encircling gulls and 'Look at them,' you said.
'They love the lighthouse. It teaches them the humility of flight.'

Precious Cargoes

Jigsaws shimmy and rattle in January beds
but nothing resolves. Just across the century
an oak-riddled well strains to listen on its hill of hopes,
but the bombers are still over the horizon.

All the old stories.

Under the city gates, how many vagabonds, magicians
will chaperone tonight the lacklustre stars no more,
how many mouths remake the fifteenth letter?

What preposterous colours, crescendos will it need
for lulled spacewalkers to lurch and turn and be astonished
by this sad stone floating in black ink like a world below?

Wait, was that the horizon rumbling?
January squeaks under the weight of thought, but dreams
are weightless, will soon evaporate in the swirling wind.

And thought will dissolve,
the jigsaws will paper it over,
and the letters mutiny, rise up, lift away from their pages
to blacken the sky. Such are the broodings of the sun,
such are the old stories.

But the bombers make the stories new again,
approaching still below the horizon. What will they do
when they arrive across the calendar,
fly into the unforgiving clouds,
the sky-black words? How will they know
where to release their precious cargoes?

January beds empty,
but every ghost that goes preserves its imprint
in the splayed pillow. Like a dream, each well runs dry,
the land. Listen. Might not the bombers bring rain?
Or will the unnumberable letters, bursting, exploding at last,
stream down on the megalopolis, smother us
under the manifold precious hills of forgotten hopes?

Boy

The tough and rumble of the schoolyard
is always welcome relief from a room
papered with whispers, where every night

he must taste the salted honey of his pain
or else listen to the chorus of lies
that they hiss at one another in the dark.

When he can't get to sleep in such dark
he gazes at where he knows the backyard
ends in a clump of wisteria – there lies

his secret, there he can shelter from his room
and pretend to escape from the pain
and pretend he isn't trembling in the night.

And he does tremble, if not every night
then at least when the inflexions of the dark
and the hissed whispers and the pain

cause him for moments to forget the yard
and listen again to the echoes that the room
so magnifies and all those ceaseless lies.

At school of course everybody lies
but brazenly, not in whispers like the night
or the bittersweet aloneness of the room

or the limpid coruscations of the dark –
it is different in the bazaar of the schoolyard
where shouts conceal the words for pain.

The wisteria grove is his refuge, no pain
can reach him there, and all the lies
melt away in that magical backyard

corner he stares into from the heart of night
where he can tangle himself inside a dark
of stubborn branches, and there is always room

for the honey of silence inside and room
for the shedding of his fear and his pain
and in those shadows he is sheltered from dark

as he sits entwined in the wisteria or he lies
prone and nuzzles to the grass until night
is ready to descend and he must leave the yard.

Must return to his room, where he lies
in his five-year-old pain waiting for night
to end, for dark to give back his backyard.

The Secret

'The impudence of man: he pretends to be alone.' (Canetti)

I saunter down the customary street,
    but nobody
can see me; I always come this way
    and no-one knows;
the housefronts with their hedges,
    regulation lawns
and leaning gables gloomy as spies
    ignore me, shrubs
look the other way, gates hold their
    breath, sprinklers
tiptoe aside, I am not here; if I stroll
    the shops or concrete
avenues it is the same, nothing detects
    my step, my shadow
alone keeps up; I hurry on, my arms
    swing, my eyes swing
and the eyes of others swing away,
    they do not see me,
I do not exist; I reach a playground
    up near the bridge,
eleven children run amongst me, they
    cannot see me too,
they clatter up the metal of a toy,
    they slither, turn
their circles as the saucer whirls
    or they swing away
just like the others; I raise an arm,
    cars divide or stop
pretending they can see me but I know
    the truth, nobody
can see me; back inside my room
    is proper honesty,

only the dressing-table mirror cheats,
    but it's a game
we have, I humour it; I like the window
    best, because I know
I am invisible and can safely watch
    myself not being seen,
relax into my creaky cane-backed
    easychair, blink
into the wind beyond the glass,
    and nobody can tell
that I exist, nobody knows I'm there;
    sometimes
there is another game I like to play
    just to make sure:
I open a window, double-hung and stiff
    from all that paint,
and lean out to the rain, letting
    my hair stream,
then rainbow my arms at whoever
    might be passing
and shout, *Look! I am here, look!*
    my lungs aflame –
and nobody knows, nobody can see;
    when I grow tired
of this I read my book, or sleep,
    or take a walk
to look for places where I haven't been,
    where nobody knows
I don't exist, where nobody yet knows
    my secret.

Riveder le Stelle

We were debating Wells & the wormhole
Time – one of those downpour days in '99, the sky
useless as a slashed umbrella, the Square indeed
from our towering Christchurch perch a mosaic
of scrabbling bats. Our poet (bleak one, he) delivered
the coup de l'argument – the old rebuttal rebus
about the boy who came back to garrotte his gramps
& reconfigure Clio. 'All lives end before their time,
Saramago says,' said he. OK, I countercut,
so what? You're blinding me with truth, take a look
at that peripathetic mob milling about down there
by the Cathedral: reckon they'd concur? 'Yeh,
some of them *are* dead, just waiting in a blur
for the Great White Light …'

                                          To this our third
but so far silent interlocutor intoned, 'I've looked
into the face of God, mah friends, & He don't exist!'
We smirked & scuttled, sucked a scotch, nibbled
on this & that. Bethissed & bethatted (verily,
a trifle sloshed), we set to spooking each other
on the other kind of coming back – 'Ah, the rebus
of re-be!' our poet cried, 'old Alighieri had birth,
rebirth & death & sex & the whole shebang
prettily down pat,' & he proceeded to mis-cite,
with fin de l'enfer glee, the Guelph into his jars:
'The heavens winking from her wormhole, thru
I came, to gape once more upon the stars!'

The Attic

'For to some degree all great texts contain their
potential translation between the lines ...'
— Walter Benjamin

I translate the books of a famous author
before they are written. It's a daunting task
that obsesses me for weeks and months at a time
until the job is done. As soon as I finish
each new volume, I store it away
in a clandestine attic high above my rooms
to which I alone have the key. There are many
such books waiting now in manuscript
along the dusty corridors of my attic,
but I never consult a single one again until
the original, in its first language, appears
in some quarter of the city. Then my real task
begins: slowly, painstakingly, line by line,
I compare my translation with the masterpiece
the great writer has published. I am never
let down — for while my translation
will correspond faithfully to the original
in syntax, orchestration, construction and sense
(not to mention vocabulary, tone and nuance)
in virtually no tangible respect, I am content
with the result, sensing always between the rows
of my laborious handiwork the truer hand
of the master — who alone would be equipped
to understand how my more perfect understanding
of his inspired words must elevate his creation
to realms even he will have feared unattainable;
and it is only his naive blend of humility and hubris,
plus the awkward reticence of genius,
which prevents him from acknowledging me
when we pass each other in the arcade, and from
clasping me with emotion to declare a truce at last.

Sanctum

So there he was in the library, crouched above the floor
     like a mousetrap, squinting into his rickety parallel edition
of the *Satires*. The paperback was from the late fifties;

its cover had long detached, released its burden, demoted itself
     to a floating flapless jacket, and some of the pages
were beginning to tip out – in short, the book required two hands

to be consulted, so his grip was intense but worshipful.
     He never journeyed anywhere without it, and he relished
the odd quotation over an ale: 'Why is it, Maecenas,'

he would mutter, 'that *no one* is ever quite happy …?'
     And there he was again, on the Persian rug, a prayermat mouse
Latining into his cups, mumbling mantras that he alone

could hear. We hated it when the demons repossessed him –
     the medicos would dismiss him as eccentric,
at best melancholic, in those days when the Sadness was just a 'cloak'.

The house tonight shook to eluctable musics, the clustered roomfuls
     jangled and rowdied onward,
distressing damsels (spilt and semiclad) drifted the liquid corridors

strumming their thighs; but he had settled himself on the magical carpet,
     Horace in hand, deaf to all temptation. A prism
of the Black Label sat beside him, the mystic flask an orange glow

on the mantel, yet his love of the elixir never placated him –
     it only made him vocal, and further classical.
Surely enough, as we broached his shadowy island he shouted: '*Nemo!*'

Kandukur

She travels across her atlas every day,
loves all the shades and shapes, the way they often
uncannily echo each other. New Zealand, for instance,
is Italy upside-down, but flopped and chopped.
Or Madagascar, sliced with a surgeon's panache
from Mozambique. Such thoughts sometimes remind her
of Kezelco, a map she could never quite follow.

The experts come, but nothing seems to change.
The monitor winks like an understanding uncle, the drip
a laconic sentinel over the bed. He used to say her voice
was a fobwatch swinging, it soothed and hypnotized;
she never really believed it. A world ago her classmates
would tease at her stutter, a childish thing she ditched
along with Ludo, but the damage was done.

She'd never told Kezelco, and never mentioned the reason
behind her 'shyness' (his awkward euphemism
that only made things worse). Three or four months, they say,
six at the most. She folds her shoulder into the too-soft pillow,
she'd like to sleep but the memories won't let her.

The channel up above flicks and flickers, the anchorwoman
brushes the wind away, some urchins crowd around her,
some helmets grin. Zoë resists the urge to listen in,
picks up the atlas again, screws up her eyes, opens a page
at random, taps a spot. Where has she landed this time?
Kandukur! *He* would have known – or galloped at once
for Google to look it up. It sounds exotic.
She must remember to ask her Indian oncologist.

Waking on the Last Morning of the Twentieth Century

31/12/2000

The eyes open at six forty-five but sink again
as the sun scrolls. From an o-nine-thirty desktop
the sky's a pneumatic blue. Will I check my email
now or next millennium? Shortly coffee,
but first scroll down the page. I hope the rising day
will justify itself, the way those grand declarations
(Jefferson, Gettysburg) extend a century's measure,
to be sifted by scribes with PageMaker manuals
questing the perfect text. Perfection's also antiquity –
the Dead Sea Scrolls, their impeccable margins.
A scroll with coffee? A thousand years scan the same
whichever way you look, echo one another
like a Strad stood up between self-regarding mirrors,
cocking the scroll of its mute infinities to listen
to the polyphony of light. The twelve-tonality of time,
its infinite variations. Old Goldberg, history-perfect:
a catalogue of endless possibilities, all the world's
tragedy and joy, the ineffable irony of music. Future?
Windows' iconology, open document. Scroll. 'A roll
of paper or parchment, usually one with writing upon it'
(*OED*). The roll of Law, a flourish under a signature,
a 'convoluted or spiral ornament', a coda or closure,
or (today's binary emblem) a floating manuscript,
Ionic, timeless, incorruptible; forever part unfurled.

Indefinite Articles

Elsternwick

A clock atick in a room
adjoining this. A sun
sprinkled through gauze
windowing day. A bird's
silence beyond & along
a street. A man
across a room from a pen
doing this. A book
under his gaze on his
upturned hand. An emptiness
around a trance. Then
                    slowly
my father lifts from a chair
to open a pane
for a breeze to riffle
a room a room
away. Returns & resumes
a book. A distant flyscreen
clangs & a pen descends
then attaches to this
again. A clock laconically
circles its dull terrain.

Malvern Interlude

for Ralph Abraham

From the speaker above, a hiphop serenade,
and from the southwest tables an endless trialogue
of anecdotal insights and narrative hype
together coalescing into noise.

But I insist on my agenda here, to cross
the fourth chapter of *Bolts from the Blue*, be taught
how Fra Angelico turned dinner-plate halos
into consummate nimbus globes.

Finishing that, I glance out the vitrine
at Claremont Avenue with its secular façades
and its pilgrims, foot-soldiers, sun-spattered vans,
while my back re-echoes its complaint:

An ache that, some days old, is not improved
by boxes of weighty books I've been manoeuvring
all over my study, courtesy of Uncle Ed,
who shuffled off and didn't take them with.

It's an impressive trove, part of it staying put,
but the majority will (I hope) insinuate
themselves onto new shelves in thankful corridors,
or living-rooms, or makers' desks –

Where nimble angels circumnavigate the heads
of scribes unborn, who wait uncertain
what they await – a fresh annunciation to hit home,
lighting up creation once again.

Her Century

Careful not to dramatize my inhibition,
I circumspied the parabola of her pearls
(Such the small consolations that define us)
While she tracked my gaze with suspicion.

Her rosary made me venture a digression:
'*You lose it if you talk about it*,' I quoted.
(Was it Günter Grass – no, earnest old Papa.)
'Let's just talk,' she converted, with compassion.

But what she wished to do was metricate me:
'You're suffering from Syndrome syndrome,'
She suggested generously. So I gambited:
'How many Texas does it take to Mississippi?'

She stared in alarm at such a liberty
(By which moment it was sixty past eleven),
Was about to triangulate a rejoinder
But thought better, so just nodded biblically,

Then grimaced and shook her hair out.
'Whatever,' she melbourned; 'first a drink –
At Young & Jackson's, a neat double-vodka.
My hundredth for the year, or thereabout.'

We dumped the tram at Federation Square,
Strolled the zebra, joined Chloe, raised our spirits.
Not unlike certain characters in the Scriptures
We went to bed, barely knew each other there.

Sin Tacks

Reason with your fingers not your fist;
Listen to the sparrow's tapdance on the floor.
When you're arguing with a needle, they a brick,
Don't forget to squat the camel, or you'll fall.

Do you fancy safety-belts for pedestrians,
Do you smear butter on both sides to be safe?
It's all in Revelation 23. It never rains
Until your holey brolly's been stashed away.

Seems to be a skill: rip what we sew.
Black is the *old* black, wish people wouldn't.
The best-planned lays will turn up nothing new,
And what we try to repeat we just redon't.

Do well, I think, to scan the grand antiquarium –
Those dusty centuries of desires, indispensable,
Wink like a crumbling lighthouse in a storm
As you founder on irony's cooling metal.

So consider that slippery old linoleum,
Seldom tango when the mopping-up's still wet.
Dim the music, assail a book, settle a stool
And rerehearse all the grammars you'll forget.

Confutatis

When I glanced inside, the old musicians were hearsing again,
somebody's Nonth Symphony, in a key impossibly remote.

This, for some odd reason, infuriated me,
and the tableau's eerie intensity implied
that I surely was unawake.

Approaching the pedestal,
I drumrolled my baton with unseemly petulance, accosted
the snowy-headed first violin, who proceeded to quote
a major Roman poet.

'*Ira furor brevis est*,' the man epistled, and grinned atrociously.

Sensing a challenge, but fancying myself
a Latinist at heart,
'*Concordia discors*,' I shot back at once. 'And what, sir, is your name?'

He streaked a thumb among unruly locks
before returning with a lazy bow, 'Why,
Tierce de Picardie, though my friends call me Quintus.
What would you have us play?'

This gave me pause, but
'Something a bit more minor,' I replied at length,
'somebody's Fifth, perhaps?'

The fiddler scratched at his scroll,
regave another of his diabolical sneers. 'Oh no,
we couldn't do that!' he nodded catachrestically, 'not unless
the work is an Opus Zero. *Nil admirari*, you know …'

(I might well have bristled at this, but my mood
had by now improved.)

With an immusical creak of knees
he regained his seat, to sound a lugubrious A.
The ragtag crew, disarranged on haphazard chairs,
ignoring me with thinly disguised wonder, shuffled
among their crossed music-stations.

Interrogatively, I upturned my palms.
'Da capo,' the ductor intoned, and they embarked
on a *Tuba mirum* by somebody not yet born.

I glanced outside, but morning was still asleep.

Jam

Sliding a slice of toast under an overlay
of margarine and jam, I'm seated solo
in an airport coffee lounge listening
to a Sonata for Accompanied Luggage
turning on a table two metres away.
The boychild (puffy with doughnut)
is throwing a mad turn, his mother turns
to unfinger a monstrous viridian ring
before not slapping him, big sister turns,
crimsonly mortified at the tantrum's key,
and looks to father's turn: he shakes
his shaven dome from behind his *Time*
and tumbles more chinotto down his throat.
They are an archipelago amid their bags
and satchels, the tide swirling around them,
as the Announcement comes. This flight
is mine. I swallow the hard crust, rise
to digest the crowd. The little larrikin,
not content with cake, is plucking at a plate
of soggy sushi, sister fends him off,
the mother curses, dad reconceals himself
behind his scarlet frame. I head into my sky.

Quest

She had told me I'd find her at the National Gallery,
    but she hadn't specified a picture. With no notion where
she might be browsing, I decided to be unsystematic and
    (hoping we had similar tastes) to revisit a few of my favourites.

To the left of the Trafalgar Square entrance were the Early
    Italian Schools, and my first stop was Crivelli's *Annunciation*;
I searched past the exaggerated perspectives, climbed
    to the background parapet above the arch, but the figures

up there chatting knew nothing of her. Entering the Sixteenth Century,
    I strolled into Giorgione's *Sunset Landscape*, questioned
a pair of saints and a passing horseman, but drew a blank.
    More than a century later, in Holland and Flanders, I stood

in Hoogh's little *Courtyard of a House in Delft*, where the girl
    waiting in the passage, her back turned, disappointed
when I glimpsed her face. On impulse I crossed another hundred,
    to the Gallery's opposite flank, and leapt into Canaletto's

illuminated heart; but the colonnades were dotted with
    idle gentlefolk, and as I traversed the piazza before St Mark's,
no passing wench in period garb betrayed *her* exquisite features.
    Sensing I'd need a sharper technique, I circled back to the doorway

and the 1800s, stopped to listen to *Music in the Tuileries Gardens*,
    mingled briefly with Manet's monochrome crowd – then repaired
to the Gallery shop. I browsed among books and pretty postcards,
    and, even though my quest had scarcely commenced, caught myself

wondering if the National *Portrait* Gallery was what she'd said.

De la Nature

Our friendship was purely aristotelian,
all ethics and poetics, but no law
to commandeer doubt or dialogue;

There was no soft agony of alternatives,
no sticky neo-nietzschean imperative,
no will to profounder cleansing;

At the time (of course) one felt quite thirty,
executor of a divine estate
amid all those tabloid rumours of demise;

We trudged colosseums of becoming,
our connectedness, more euclidean now,
still kindled a stern metaphysic;

Though at last (the universe cooling)
one noticed the global glow
that wriggled from the tar-line up ahead;

And made haste placidly – was it not
just around the corner of a page,
nearly there, we were treading time;

Our friendship grew quaintly cartesian,
all seven-way mirrors and equations,
and we flirted with dialogue and doubt;

We unravelled the pascalian dialectic,
reconsidered the purity of the vowels,
understudied the logics of arrival;

But innocent of what awaited here,
we exulted in the chorus and the comedy,
wading forward, forever quite thirty.

My Wattle Princess

The twin steeples of the Cathedral stood out
above the treeline like stern monitors. Slotted along
neat channel-paths between the flowerbeds,

steel longchairs sat, brown question-marks,
their ribs curvatured into reposing valets and dames,
some elderly, some just old-at-heart, logging-in

perhaps to each other's parkside fantasies
or lipreading the lurid pockets of orbiting joggers.
As good a day as any, and better than some;

but to one soul, seated beside a lone Cootamundra,
a remote, unreadable day. Indifferent she
to the dim cavalcade – and to this suspect co-sitter

studying her with fabled nonchalance
opposite, next to a trim plantation of forget-me-nots.
No signal hers of any inkling or unease, no

scruple of desire to modulate to a remoter key –
still as a stone, her sock-striped ankles
loosely crossed, black jeans under a purple blouse

beneath a cardigan covered by a coat, boots black,
and any unexpected bonnet or a cap
missing from the reddish crop encircling her brow.

I have long lowered my volume to my lap
(*The Saxon and Norman Kings*, Christopher Brooke)
to memorize again that shadowy processional –

Egbert through Æthelstan to the Confessor Saint –
but I cannot turn back the gentle wavelets
lapping at me across the pebbled sand: I find myself

oddly imprisoned by this remorseless girl I fancy
as some fallen princess hard at conceiving
her glorious reinvention or revenge – for alongside

that statelessness (it appears no less), a grand serenity
seems to command her features, and her eyes,
almost incomprehensibly, *shine* like a state of grace;

and despite the respectable pathway that divides us,
I want to stand, approach, be granted audience,
for I have now resolved she is a Queen, and could

with one breathtaking regal tremble of her wrist
reduce me to my knee to drop my head
and learn the tingle of her sceptre at my neck;

and as I arise, her eyebrow too will lift,
ever so slightly, o sweet conspiracy, to let me know
she will be waiting in her chamber at twelve …

But then, instead, she coughs – a shocking cough,
so rasping and infernal that I jump; then, scowling,
crisply flips a consummate one-finger salute

out of her garbled sleeve, spits out across our moat
a crude if ambiguous suggestion; and then –
she stood, brushed herself down, and hobbled off

in the direction of the stern Cathedral. And me, I fled:
back to my patient history, back to exiled
Unready Æthelred, wily Canute, his relentless sea.

Ark

one heaven hurls its arrows in the gloom.
one writhing sea released from the burden of land.
one planet newly oceaned in liquid death.
one teeming stinging firmament opaque.

animals wait.

unabating waters pummel the slippery boards.
the superstructure creaks.
he gazes out.
something is idling blackly on his brain.
he challenges again the sky to conjure wings.
too many days already too many days.

animals wait.

his wife his sons and daughters lie asleep.
he scans convex horizons like a man.
he must imitate those that will follow.
too many days.
they shadow one another like a curse.
is there no respite from the jaws of faith.
he watches for a signal seeks a sun.
maybe its warmth will penetrate his soul.
his words surround a prayer that will not come.

animals stir.

one sudden cloudlet dissipates and there.
within.
a small silhouette flies.
no green thing dangles from its beak.

animals wait.

the superstructure groans.
one sky reflects.
he waits.
the vessel pitches in the gathering calm.
one sliver lodges in his pulse like pain.
he must imitate those that will follow.
one song hovers like poison on his blood.
a covenant he cannot forsake.
the bird becomes a circling diadem.
the timber slopes under his callused feet.

animals wait.

he reaches deep into the black behind the eyes.
this bird must not abandon them again.
now he knows.
he must imitate those that will follow.
he lifts the crossbow.
aims.
lowers it slowly as the arrow uncanny arrives.

Once We Crossed the Equator

Once we crossed the Equator
we understood that we could never turn back
for all the seabirds were flowing in the opposite direction
and the disturbance we created
in the air and on the water was always behind us
the sea an endless terrain of low peaks and ranges
rising, falling, rising until snow broke out on their crests
the breeze awash with a strange exhausted vibrancy
the motors' throbbing below us a dull obbligato
the portholes clear and free of reflections
for the sun too was behind us
and if not behind us then asleep somewhere
behind the clouds with their fantastical topography
through which glimmers of naive colour remotely whispered

When we crossed into the Tropics
the light changed, and suddenly the vessel's surfaces
its polished timbers and quaint panelling
took on a novel sheen, peculiar images appeared
at first faint effigies of memories we had not yet dreamed
then gradually colours and curves that intoxicated
the more we attached our hungry gaze to their geography
and we knew we would need to possess them
and we knew we never could
because the seabirds and the clouds
and the engines' low insistence told us so

As we crossed into the Polar regions
we discovered we could no longer discern the birds
the water became mere ripples
like the breath of a sleeping infant
the air had lifted and the clouds assumed a snowy radiance
it was colder here of course

but there were rumours that the sun was expected
that the mechanical hum would be stilled
that the brittle ice rising, falling, rising around us
until the pieces joined and fused into each other
would slowly melt and sink
amid all the other prophecies of our past

and we could proceed in silence
unencumbered by dreams and imaginings
our horizon shining and almost touchable beyond
our vessel's lengthening shadow
towards the Equator

The Sky-Tree

On an island just south of the future we discovered
a tree that grows downward from the sky.
We could not conceive in what manner of sky-soil
its roots might be set, nor how it could stay
suspended thus, scarce beyond reach of urchins
and adventurers who would surely have tried to scale it
out of sheer impudence, or to unearth its secret,
lost in clouds of the forbidden past.
Beneath its broad inverted canopy, children
would gather mushrooms and paint magic scenes
with rainbow colours pressed from iridescent globes
that lay about, ripe droppings of the Sky-Tree,
as it was called by the wagoners who would trundle by,
delivering candlesticks to the village across the river –
their voices lit up in reciprocal greeting when we
waved excitedly, and they would dismount
with tender anecdotes of homelands beyond the hills.
One, especially, used to steal spirited glances
at my precocious sister, who, not unaware
of her fragrant allure, would puff out her cheeks
and strut about under the Sky-Tree's disapproving gaze:
her antics pitched the yokel to such gusts of laughter
and desire that once, as he chased her through the filigrees
of his own shadow, his soul, trailing in the breeze,
caught the tip of a sky-branch swaying sternly
as if to protect the virgin, and the great tree gave out
a shudder so regretful that the earth grew dim
under a carpet of cascading memory,
and we could swear the sky itself was about to tumble.

Full Moon, Thebes

(Ozymandias speaks)

One night, a thousand calendars from now,
A traveller from some godforsaken land
Will tremble here, under the midnight hour,
And wonder at the elemental hand
That could lift up such testaments to power
And splendour and eternity: he'll stand
Craning his mind at this colossal work,
Made dizzy by the desert stretching round,
And my stone visage will enlight the murk
With histories that sing, as they astound,
The might of Rameses and his dominion;
And if he scan his books, he will despair
At one ungrateful race that sought Oblivion –
How Pharaoh let them go, and left them there.

Denizen

I sit in a room with my face to the door,
No trust in the world outside;
I dream of above and I long for below,
My room is both narrow and wide.

The enemies gathering beyond the gate
Of the city are patient and shrewd;
So I sit with my back to the wall and I wait
In my dark, indeterminate mood.

I could equally ask you to stay at my side
Or abandon me to my devices;
And I'm weary of waiting, of having to bide
My time with my satchel of vices.

But I'll answer unhesitatingly
Should you question my quarantine home –
I sit with my face to the door and I see
The sky's indecipherable dome

From a window that tells me the time of day
And confirms me in my decision:
That the globe may be spinning but I must stay
My course with unmeasured precision.

Semper Fidelis

When he grew tired of his model railway,
the stamp collection in twelve hefty albums,
and the telescope through which he followed
unseemly events in the tenth-floor bedroom
directly across from his, the Director would
retire into his library, windowless and glowing
from a Doric sconce columned at each wall,
there to rotate his armillary sphere, watching it
spin and tilt the globe-encrusted firmament
within the mystic drama of its geometry, there
to finger the blade of the gilt letter-opener
from his Gibraltar uncle (or an aunt in Spain)
its handle illustrated with erotic scenes and
scored in Cyrillic 'to a fond opener of letters'
during the previous century. Such oblique
objets deliberated there – a cut-glass egg-timer
from Tashkent; a buddha, fist-sized but solid
as half his whole Macaulay (1864); a shard
from a vase Keats might well have fondled,
legacy of an elderly Cracovian; a piano-roll
of a patriotic J. P. Sousa march ... And there,
his volumes pressing from behind their bars,
he could plan in peace how best to deracinate
the next most urgent enemy of the state.

Microcosmos

From the one-way automatic sliding-doors
to the Visitors' Book is a two-metre ravine
of thirty years. I sign in. The red-headed shuffler
in his grimy captain's cap hovers near the desk
as always, the lobby chairs are filled as always
with alerted eyes that have witnessed
the best, the worst the world can show. I stroll
past these asylum-seekers from my own century,
the one we left behind a decade back, the one
strewn with promises and tombs, the one
that tossed up its fervent supplications
into depleted skies that uttered steel, stone, smoke,
and the mocking echoes of a faith hallowed
and hollowed by three thousand winters. The one
whose alphabet spent itself, that nomad's-land
of language harbouring a wilderness of words
drained of habitat, notes without melody, light
without shade, only shadow. They follow
my tread, these still-embodied spirits, the one
that sits with a Mesmer's gaze (who used to dance
in the salons of Petersburg), the one ready
to do battle to protect her armchair by the door
(hidden by a farmer in Silesia, two dozen months
swallowing scraps and cellar dust), the one
who stares suspicious at what moves, trembles
his magazine with a melancholy gleam, or one
hunched in a loop like her conversation, repeating
the same question to each visitor, her grateful grin
at the answer (who watched her family crumple
under an Auschwitz fence, a cornflower sky).
With feigned authority I march toward the lifts,

and the sense that enfolds me now is not of pity
but a kind of joy – a crazy unfiltered *yes*,
the gorgeous pulse and vanity of what clamours
to be alive, still and in spite of all, and living,
even in this foreshortened microcosm of time.

The Steeples

So we continued into the valley of ruined machines
Weaving our trace among the blackened wreckage
The charred distillations of our wizardry and love

We hummed chorales and inhaled the death-smoke
Curling from the steeples in the wavering distance
And we wondered at the implacable grey thunder

The birthquake of the proliferating generations
Who would curse our dim elegance and engineering
The conceits we had nailed upon this landscape

And all the while our machines gazed up at us
Though we had long ceased searching the quiet sky
For a sign of grace or music in the skeleton trees

So what use the rust we scrabbled against rudely
Or the clay-crusted levers we unearthed to rekindle
The wheels and pulleys that had taunted eternity

We failed of course so we hoisted our memories
Blew the powder of sleep from our bulging histories
Endured a night of tacit copulations and proceeded

She

Now more than ever seems it rich to die ...

She came to me delicately robed
resting her staff behind the rickety bookcase
draping her black beret
from the corner skeleton stand

I thought I might be meant to embrace her
but there was a flint of warning in her eye
and her mouth was pursed
so I turned back to my designs

She curled her lean ampleness
into the folds of the couch in the corner
and the settle of her gown rustled softly
and I sensed the season ripen

I glanced up now and then
distracted momently by her sculpted profile
her melancholy calm
and her now exquisite mouth

She was at silence though
all discretion and silence
and as the old clock grew dizzy
she nodded agreeably once that's all

I looked up (it was twilight)
and she was gone
but when I turned back to my designs
she was perched on the edge of my desk

She was older than I had thought
I observed curiously
and she was younger also
and her rich mouth was moist

I looked about the room
the clock was in shadow
the window curtained for the night
the couch draped in darkness

She let her purple garment drop away
from glossy shoulder sleek hinterland
she pulled back the bedclothes
and for the first time smiled

Suddenly I was with her
about her upon her
I was claiming my bounty
I sensed her body open delicately

She took me then
and when next I looked out onto my room
I could see nothing
night had finally fallen

I drifted toward my desk
searched in vain for the lamp
while she lay languid and replete
ready for her reward

What the Dead Do

The dead have their own tasks. (Rilke)

Certainly they do not ride the ghost-trains
    or scale the clifftops deliberating Dante;
They have lost their taste for old gothic
    or the peerless glaze of the Renaissance,
And they soon disremember the sinfonias
    or motets in memory's overtones,
While the fading watermarks of their existence
    or its lingering traces they cling to
Keep receding like some flimsy recollection,
    or a pen that must erase as it writes;
And they have noticed a strange deliquescence,
    or it seeps about them like an ether –
That they no longer recoil from one another
    or peer beneath bridges in disquiet,
No longer need resemble their unlikenesses
    or adjudicate the maxims they lived by;
They grow heedless of hurt and pleasure
    or the multicoloured stations of the mind,
Having shed the sideshow nightmares
    or bolted reawakened from their slumber;
And the impulse to craft and curiosity
    or the itch to scrape at the unbearable,
Because suddenly stilled, is jettisoned
    (or transmuted like quicksilver to sand)
So at last they can empty and be copious,
    or encompass the silentness of attuning
To their new dispensation which is Eternity,
    or Time's true unendurable meaning.

The Last Word

On the day the last word was used up
we scoured the streets, combed the countryside,
desperate to locate another. We sensed
only remotely the purpose to which we might put it,
yet understood that the alternative
was unthinkable. So much had already
become unthinkable, as we struggled to retain
our composure in the novel darkness
that had drifted onto the land
when the last word vanished. Who now
was to say what the coming days would reveal?
It was difficult to believe, deep down,
that no word would ever again disclose itself,
but as we searched, a seeping despair
colonized our hearts, like a colourless ink
staining our knowledge across a land
arid and thirsty for – what?
There was no describing this desolation,
no adequate gesture, no touch, no simile fresh
from the realm of thought, just a melody
circling the unaccustomed dark,
burning its song into a speechless sky.

from *The Rearrangement*

(1988)

A Concise History of the Moon

'for the moon is never but a month old ...'
— *Love's Labour's Lost*

I *Full*

She crosses herself
the old woman. Night after night
one blind sleepwalker can recall nothing
of the sun. And when she opens her eye wide
she is drifting
anciently, a ball of bone with a lid
on the blackening future. She smiles, almost
like a great grandmother
in her private particular satisfactions
or an infant at the telescope's opposite end
propped up among her sandbox computations
stacking time.

II *Waning crescent*

If you look up
If you consider what it is you have lost
If you frame the disc like a metaphor through a spyglass
    fondle it like a warm marble in your palm
    pronounce it like a mantra rounding your tongue
If you look up and consider
    the breeze of ice crossing the night into your lashes
    and stripping
    open your mouth to the distances between you
    and close your eyes
    and make love to the breeze that no longer knows you
Trying to remember
Trying to remember the moon and the silence of the moon
    and open your touch to an ancient fear
    shoving hard against its womb

Trying to recall
>why the birth to be will shut forever
>this chamber you have scratched your lifetime into

Trying to recall so much
>and so much more beyond recalling

If you do all this
>and still count yourself a survivor
>and expose your eye to the swivelling moon
>and smile
>and swing your face into the clock behind you
>always behind you

If you do all this
>you will have conquered the invisible again
>you will probably turn and cross the blustering moor
>and forget the old-woman moon
>fidgeting peacefully above you
>always above you

You will forget that a moon was once your mandala
>forget the fear
>return to the cities of the morning smouldering in their history
>rebuilding themselves as they have always done
>relearning all the orthodox betrayals
>recalling
>the slumbering creatures from their caverns under the heart
>and the world will go on

If you do all this
>and nothing will have changed
>only the moon
>like a mother you have sacrificed forever
>crossing herself night after night

And you will forget as you have always forgotten
>even if you remember
>even if you pause to recall the song of an ancient woman
>even

If you look up

III *New*

Every dome we built is overgrown with tendrils,
They say the time to civilize our satellite
    Is coming soon;
Architects and doctors, planners with their pencils
    Design and theorize and calibrate
        For living-room.

Thinking stops the blood, a mounting terror festers,
The leaving of a land is no small sacrifice
    Even for us;
Seldom in the drunkest dreams of our ancestors
    Could such an odyssey have been devised
        We dare at last.

Trapped between the smell of history and stasis,
We plot a future where forgetfulness will cross
    The crescent Earth;
Children we encounter (ours or something else's)
    Will seek in vain within their glossaries
        The word for birth.

IV *Waxing gibbous*

Sometimes your face would be the imprint
                on a secret letter
meticulously folded. Sometimes you were legible,
                just – like an alphabet
at the bottom of a pool, or a poet
                teen-eyed but beginning to turn
to a don with a beard scanning every row
                with suspicion. Sometimes
you'd vanish with a scoundrel's tact, or look
                the other way – as when a schoolboy
stuck on a cricket-field discovered something
                in his pocket. And
while you flooded his volumes on the topmost shelf,
                friends in high places
sometimes pressed balcony railings waiting for you,
                their dark drives
mapped out like old Verona, the lamp
                at the top of the rickety lane
a cliché but a backseat compass. Your beam
                for the first was a firefly's newel,
for the second a cable inviting incredible men
                to devise footfalls. But
you – you were always the silent type, Asian
                for all the centuries of rhetoric,
your face creased like a careless page …
                Today the distances
behind a face unfold into the infancy of moons.
                To remove the crease from a letter
it is necessary sometimes to refold it.

V *Full*

My bed is relentless.
The blanket squats about an upraised knee,
my pillow is whistling in my ear.
The rectangle I'm regarding from a small distance
holds back the window-frame.
There could easily be a curtain:
    there is no curtain.

The sky is incontinently blue
somewhere to the west; here
there's a dark side being enacted.
On the cubical bedside table a timepiece
glints like a handcuff draped for dead
but coming, coming – the four zeros of midnight:
    I close my eyes to hold them.

In truth the sky outside is navy black.
If I looked into it
through the window's phlegmatic tunnel
I could arrest the ooze of a cloud.
This notion seduces: at the point of no return
the corner of her eye
    hooks on to mine –

The moon ... A ringtail
chronically entangled in the beams above
scrapes like a tedious thought,
a spiteful motorcyclist lacerates the night:
glissandos unsettle me –
I think of sirens, the wailing
    of the ghost train to Treblinka,

Craters of an unseen topography ...
I think of what I have never lost,
I float out through the ceiling like Chagall
and peruse the village, a tablecloth
into the past. I measure
ten thousand years of dripping candlewax
    wasted, burnt in vain.

And I hear the slide of the logical ocean
of seconds, centuries, crushing
the cry from the throat of logicians.
I weigh the heft of an axe, its logic;
the twig treason of a doddering pencil.
I taste the black olive of a love
    lapping at its bitter stone self.

And I listen to animals under the roof
drunken for crumbs, discover a map
riddled with daggers crossing into the distance.
I am dizzy from lusts
accomplished in the name of blood, flesh,
Eternity:
    they swirl before me like stars ...

And the moon:
the crazy circle's fleeting symmetry
between the boards of the bedroom I return to.
It is crossed again by the swim of vapours
older by far than any Tranquil Sea:
and it melts into my mouth.
    I sleep, and dream of light.

Cyril and the Snails

Cyril, sixty, alone,
rams cussing clear through
the slack back door paunching the flyscreen
wide with his convexity;
the accustomed slap
will spring the screen right back upon its flap.

Cyril, solitary, prone
to attacks of lethargy and flu
stumbles on split half-lit lino mat grumbling
his grope for beer and a smoke;
chestful of hair
flattens to a slump in his easy-chair.

Cyril, content, alone,
guzzles wincing old sweat anew –
the dozen snails his boot stepped dead tonight
furrow the bristles of a grin;
his chaotic jaw
reconstructing shell-cracks listens to a war.

Cyril, wounded, prone
in a ditch drinks fear through
from a life waged an age ago, shudders awaking
cold to his concavity
one ache to another;
these days he never thinks about his mother.

Stokes a cigar – enjoys to tap and send
and watch the ash fall neatly from its end.

The Composer on his Birthday

I am thirty-five: next year Wolfgang
   will be dead. Young Franz lies buried in Vienna now
      three seasons under. Even the infant Arriaga's no doubt

notched his genius. High time for Hochzeit
   is the needle of an ailing mother, she spies
      a grandchild round every corner but I remain deaf

dreaming my firebirds & kalevalas, or a father of twenty who
   still had time. Already mirror-scratched, I'll soon be scored
      as the grim sheets grinning back, edentulous with

missed music: my curlicues stare bleak at the decay
   around them, tracked by a thin fate. What should have been
      the great romance of Chroma & Diaton is an Opus 1

Allegro fragment scattered lovesick
   on slippery timber. I sit to excavate knowing all musics
      are entrapped in this ivory but the keys

lie tacit, unbroken – neat bones of a cryptic enigma
   the solutions to which are infinite are
      impossible are at worst

satisfactory. Sebastian is smiling like a steep uncle, Bonn's
   mountain pulsates with laughter. My mother
      is weeping.

I must journey once more to Vienna.

A Song at Last

You were short on luck that year:
you, and the lean city of a monstrous Bridge
about to meet halfway.

I recall you had no hat, I'd catch you shivering
for our stealthy rendezvous behind
backyard beds

of grass and fishbone fern. But a style: struck up
or shouldered, exquisitely forlorn – this
you possessed in measure.

I can't pretend we ever shared an intimacy
or plotted to reach each other,
but those half-light

Sunday shadowplays through paling fences by
cat-alley scrawn-shapes in the dusk
drove home

my inescapable aloneness as no mirror-mirror
coming clean could have.
We lost each other in our sad and frantic dance

and found no solace Monday could afford
to taint us with – yet by Thursday was the throb,
that delicate lightheaded

madness rising once again, and I'd stash
a world in every paling gap along the Balmain
rundown alleypaths

laughing inside me. Soon Sunday, and a churning
breathless song maddened in my blood,
a song at last.

An Intelligent Conversation

    Arranging meanings more or less concisely,
      My glass a shell-game on the wood,
I sit across from you and what you're thinking
    And what you understand me to be saying
        (The way I sense my words misunderstood)

    Knowing already more or less precisely
      The labyrinthine morning and the good
That none of it can do me, but unblinking
    Barging ahead because the game we're playing
        (Depending on the way the game is viewed)

    Narrows all choices down to this. Nicely
      We nestle in the sway of wine – the gentle hood
I've lowered on our studious drinking
    You cannot hope to spot: this smarting, staying
        (As I so surely, swiftly knew it would)

    Sudden panic of words, the icily
      Ascending ache of too much said. I brood,
I mean the half or quarter of me sinking,
    On this, or the reverse: of not displaying
        (Or not in time, or not the time I should)

    Sufficient eloquence. Surprisingly
      We dwell on drawn remarks about the food –
But I, in pain, already feel the slinking
    Triffids of my redemption ramifying
        (Prowling our topic's rocky neighbourhood)

      Waiting the chance to pounce, then, crazily
    To wrench the dialogue back where it had stood
Back where it hurts: a frenzied linking
    Of the dead and the forever dying
      (Words, phrases, clauses, whole sentences unglued)

      For what? ... A wisdom snatches at me. Wisely
    Or not the fractions must yield. I think you'd
Be astounded at my agony, what with claret clinking,
    Close in a way. I abdicate, delaying
      (If not discarding what cannot be renewed)

      The rigours of post-mortem till the night. I see
    Dark armies waiting: border-lines are crude
And sanity's the quintessential hubris ... Blinking
    Smoke aside, the edges of my panic slowly fraying
      (In my own way, replenishing my mood)

      I leave the past, letting the moment prise me
    Gently away (you'd never notice it). The wood
We lean against is slowly shrinking,
    Meanings resume: claret and speech allaying
      The anticlockwise cannot into could.

Into the Heart Again

for Ruth

It is at such times that I would want
to slip sideways into the mist
like an open disentangled envelope
floating down in gentle, careless
zigzag arcs, a paper leaf dropping back
from autumn, back toward the source,
leaving the ochre season high behind, high
in the world of three dimensions.

Collecting my life in books that spine
these cubical perimeters, I scan
the magic-lantern glow from the soft focus
of a swivelling chair, elbows desked,
feet awake, waiting. Any moment now
I shall let them glide – the grey
complacent carpet will respond, grip, draw me
away from half-formed half-felt thoughts.

It is at such times that I would need
to pour downwards onto the page
like an open dripping melon, the black wet seeds
bursting into syllables, their ink
the blood of exploding kaleidoscopes: to spatter
the bookcases, splash black and crimson truth
over the bleached leaves of print – paper
cutouts for all their four-dimensioned

secret odysseys. To splash back into my eye:
from there to trickle richly, lovingly,
ineluctably, into the heart again.

Wondernight

for Zofia Radwańska

1

I was a child
when a picture book
brought me this/

a study
dark among its panels
the household

asleep/ a pendulum
somewhere
softly clicks/ midnight

Suddenly
bookshelves stir/ the books
are coming to life

they wake/ start
to converse/ glide or file
to the floor

begin a vigorous
debate/ each volume utterly
unlike the next

It is a wondernight
of books
the room vibrates/ colours

& covers throb
pages windmill/ a dance
of books

that should have stayed
the shelf
where day belongs

2

Try to recatch
the colour of that tale
I fell for/

find
I can almost
close my memory

around it
almost/ stubborn is the
old steep

impossibility
to be a little boy
again

3

Dwindling
the night gives notice
to return/

the books
must reinstate a front
for the sun

a facade/ for morning
to discover
perfect order/ shelves

repossessed
the spines & sequences
restored

4

And I wish
that I could hold this
Polish fable once

more in my hand/ protectively/
lest by the colour
it no longer

lent/ the flaws
in the text
& the art

I picked at/
these books should finally
close their dream

& I/ unreconciled/ resume
my book
to book search for myself

Springvale

In the city of the dead
with my mother. Necropolis
is many cities:

they float amid
the listening geometry & I
said things

not said
when they could have been said
& saw shapes.

My father
slowly closed his back to the
shut earth, & I

drifted ahead,
pausing to browse among
names

& sealed numbers
as they led me quietly
stone to stone

endward. I
among the rows imagined
absent mourners'

thoughts, hovering
low like abandoned clouds:
each belonging

silent to a silent
seldom-revisited mirror
in the ground.

Elsternwick

In the rooms of the living the others
    kept their distance.
My father sat stone-tired, lulled
    by the kitchen light
beneath an exhausted silence, drained
    hollow & lost in focus.

Her room belonged to me,
    our second-last secret. I hovered
in & out many times
    like an anxious parent, my mind
bone-dry, the moments
    collected, even now. She peaceful
as tired stone, cool to my touch, asleep
    almost. Told her my heart.
Noted how readily, how calm I kept
    returning to sit by her, how I kissed
the still cheek, how clearly
    I commuted between her room &
the real world.

    It was not until later,
not till I tasted the orphan
    remnants of her very last cake, crafted
with a heart joyful & failing,
    that the tears came.

Our very last secret.

Optical Illusions

I *Snapshots*

They visit seldomer now, they object
    to obligation. Her quirks are like a rock
they recoil from turning to the light. Embarrassed
    silences embarrass them, patience is an act
they're proud to be past. They believe in old people's
    homes and separate children's bedrooms. Once
they stood indistinguishable but decades
    of estrangement have damaged each facsimile. Twins,
they still connote dim jealousies, itch from
    the cuneiform jibes of a late luckless mother. Dad
they detest: he dawdles these days in a premature garden
    flogging dead campaigns, promising
they'll never know a thing about The World. They live
    18 streets apart. They were born on D-Day.

He kills the candles – youngest of 3
    reminds smutty celebrants '56 was The Year:
he invokes the Olympics, the Box, the Rockers,
    Budapest, Suez (the twins grow drunker);
he drops in passing Pakistan's crescent, *The Ten*
    Commandments, Castro's coming – and wait!
he remembers the Utzon Opera, the palace of
    Emperor Diocletian … (they leave). At work
he's been working on Wendy, or studies the clock
    like Kafka; Sundays he sketches or
he does the odd poem, puzzles through chess and
    Zen meditation. He longs to believe
he despises uranium. Insane some nights he
    curls up and cries; could never kill himself.

She was born 1900, New Year's
    morning. On occasion
she's promised to catch the '90s –
    never 2000, 'wrong millennium'
she giggles (drunken cicadas clamour):
    her 85 summers sparkle like radium,
she glows in the bask of delicate
    hauntings. On occasion
she tires of the postcard cottage, the
    rugs unsteady, the smell of time;
she remembers less of the last 20 years,
    her mind grown musty, 'rewinding'
she whispers: a carpet The War
    at the root of its tongue.

II *Mirror*

My guilts are not what suicide is made of.
I sit and cling
like a crab to the glossy years,

they hold me back: the looking-glass behind me
alters, clouds
like a wineglass when I appear.

If I should listen it will seem to sidle closer,
grow silent, somewhat
invisible, then whisper: You see,

I give you the universe, emptied and anticlockwise,
and still you prefer
your impossible phantoms to me ...

So I suffer the sin of Orpheus. My music
offers me childhood,
sweetmeats, lust, cyder and sleep;

but the sky still hovers and humbly announces
its mission, whenever
star-spiders fashion their winding sheet.

And I find I utter the curse of ten thousand winters
(I crab the glass,
a godlessly pacing pilgrim): The pain of

the future's a luxury that can't be afforded,
today is enough.
The world will be up to our children ...

III *Eyes*

Sometimes I catch myself with my mother's eyes:
I sense my features mention for a moment
her face still waiting deep within me. Time
swallows its tail ... Child, they say it is my wife
you mirror. Maybe so. Yet in the richness of a cliché
I detect at moments equally rare
my mother again, trapped in *your* eye.

                                Look at you:
your helpless trusting sleep rips at my spirit
like a kind of guilt. You were born
where Continental shadows run tangent to the soil;
our elders, exiles from a war they think
they survived, wait like a stalled procession; and I sit
crosslegged in the safelight, watching.
So it goes. The centuries of Europe
lean out across us from the hills beyond, and
the ravines within – unless we presuppose a universe
senile and shabby ...

                Two years old:
I watch you till it hurts. I nod,
I snatch what sleep is left on offer,
I huddle on the floor, your hand clutching at mine
between thin bars of cot.
                      What fears
already prowling on your eyes
ignite to make you cry out in the dark?
What ogres plod the village of your mind,
stubborn reflections of my own stale ghosts …?

                    Hold on to me tight,
little girl. We have little more this moment
than each other.

Lines from the Horizon

I

Next door they were burying Stalin.
I pencilled swastikas on awkward bombers tongue
between my teeth. I am speaking loosely but
this was crime: so flagrant an abuse

of kindergarten privilege wrenched my parents
to the scene of it, where clean-day custodians
flourished the evidence. I suppose mum and dad
pleaded bemusement, smiled excuses

and as the strange irony floated before them
like icing on waves barely now receding, slowly
ebbing back to outline the dozen incomprehensible
years of murdered families and smashed lives

the reprimand must have rankled a good deal more
than mine. Poland 1953 and Adolf Hitler lay
unburied: not for my public elucidation these
twisted symbols glimpsed in forbidden books.

*

I am speaking loosely.
If Germany remained the black sign, grey glinting
square head of steel, Russia was crimson banners
and gold echo of sad brass dulled by static.

We heard the funeral live from Moscow:
I hogged the wireless by the armchair corner
listening keen, for though I understood little enough
of the world I knew the great leader

from First of May parades and tabloid portraits.
My father for that matter had forged his own
passing acquaintance: idealist up to the close
of those dim thirties he fled to Utopia for a brief

quick comedown as the other vision sprawled east
to enweb him and history. Years later he recalled
a friend from the clamorous decade who'd invested
generously in Polish jails for professing Marx,

had stumbled at length across the promised border
to redeem his prize – retired on it too, ended
his days proverbially: a dead 'counterrevolutionary'
in Siberia. My father was luckier at Mauthausen.

History keeps doing it to us doesn't it!
A faith becomes a tourniquet – sallow believers
choke on lean principles, time sniggering ... Well,
petrol bombs and Sputniks soon made up for Stalin.

*

America? Colourless; also red-and-white
tins of Carnation milk. I loved to stack and clatter
and roll them on the cool floor, precious
from brown parcels and faraway benefactors.

They needn't have come from America. Canada then?
Or maybe even Australia ...

*

Australia was simply vague distant relatives, and
Olympics. Melbourne and 1956. I remember
tank pictures – but another image: from stamp album
afternoons survives the green chunky lushness of

Collins Street, trammed, treelined, dense
with colour boldly printed. I'd never seen this
vividness in stamps; even the Hungarian were
pastels by comparison. Special stamp,

like the special tablecloth I watched my mother
embroider with special songs, happy patterns
of flower and paisley while dad quizzed me with maps
and capitals, foreign letterheads on stamps.

*

No such colours in the steelworks
of my steel city's environs or in the coalmines,
in the black pits of my and not-my soil. I must admit
they belonged to me for a time:

when the coalminers came to kindergarten to sell
Poland, their black-and-red ceremonial uniforms
stunned me with golden buttons, plumed caps,
looming strength – granite, heroism, and

a dignity so persuasive I determined
to shovel coal when I grew up and for close hours
we laboured with clag and scissors, black card
and red tissue assembling cylindrical hats

young patience fired, novel patriotism fed
by smallness and the will to height, to meaning.
I brought mine home, it fell apart and left my life
for other shades to fuel preoccupation.

*

And other colours we had in abundance: chimneys
of steel and soot were never near enough
to stain our days. We had parks with statues,
flowers in my city, tones and scents that inscribed

on memory forever. Katowice was fresh
as Olympic Melbourne on Sunday park excursions ...

*

In Park Kościuszko – no,
not your Snowy Mountains upstart size of all Poland
but a tract of the native genus in white Katowice –

we toboggan, dad and I, scraping
the mad slopes and chill morning swirls our breath
asperging laughter. Then the bathos of short stopping

or noisy glee of rude wreckage, and the trudge
upward again, and again. Beyond see-through trees
and slightly adrift in cloud

winters the dim parachute tower, hardly today
the cynosure of Junes and towering summers, solitary
cold in its private public clearing.

*

In Park Kościuszko, then,
on a summer's dogtail day I waggle my fresh bicycle
not entirely steady on my first bicycle day.

Concluding homeward out of park my confidence
grown more reckless now and caution thrown dozing
(there is no wind) I can wobble alone,

soon jettison my father's jogging saddle hand
to thread him and mum proudly out behind and wheel
solo into the downhill Sunday promenade

alongside park perimeters. Downslope, gathering pace,
freewheel and hair teeming ... down – till the sudden
query dawns: how do you stop? But weaving

through strollers, defeating cars now that cruise
safe on the parallel way I panic stopless,
any brakes forgotten or unlearnt, bear down, cross

with a bump the promenade finish, run the car-strung
intersecting street handlebar stiff and held
only by miracle and terror from spilling or being

collected, jump the far footpath, burst
a gateway at thirty or so, and in an utterly
unheard-of manner vault up a flight of stairs my bike

still under me, pale parents closing. I sit there
unseated and unscathed. I'm recollecting loosely:
except for landing up the stairs it is all true.

II

But I was going to speak of Australia.
These random isolated crests of reminiscence ebb
slowly back now to outline the irreplaceable decade,
sufficient setting. It was my first childhood,

kaleidoscope I'd need more than poems and pages
to review. For the moment let me find myself
in my tenth year on the Rose Bay Public doorstep
days post arrival with nor bike nor tongue

for buttress, classified Alexander: fair translation.
It is 1958 with kindly classmates but weeks
before I glean sense in their mannered declamations
from *School Magazine* or can frownlessly decipher

the laws of Mister Jones. At playtime, lunch and
of a morning you can venture marbles: 'Hit one
win four!' and variants are among my first English
songs in the raucous bazaar of gleaming teeth

and taws. Forget your parallelograms
of economic forces: *here* the nerve-roots of capital,
education. Arrive mornings modest pouches clicking
investment, go home packed pockets bulging

or downcast broke. And so the solemn frenzy
is thick until the bell, or till the proud bass drum
and keen recorders fall in for the daily march,
then the Lord's Prayer *en masse*. And as for me

I am small, not unsheltered, bespectacled, foreign:
already I am weaving private fantasies.

*

When I say foreign (and I am speaking loosely)
I mean the time between arrival and the shedding
of doubt face to face. With facility for language
and youth on side I proceeded briskly:

harder for my parents – whole cultures to unlearn,
unravel, beyond the jawbreak diction, perversities
of mad spelling, impossible grammar. This,
and then communicate. It's an art to inhabit

the vernacular Australia from within; finer art
if you've abandoned much more than a decade
anchored elsewhere. Key, unlocker of open gates
to the great anonymous society, this dialect is

world: not the fighting earthiness of Polish yards
or the urgent grit of Israel I managed to assume
in a year-long interlude, second childhood of
another day's tale. No, I am speaking of Australian:

the virile easy gambit, a calm logistics of dialogue,
something precious and tacit, cool as choreography

and warm as dance. Found in taxis, gloomed corridors
of swish Glebe terraces, Toorak rose gardens

no less than in dim bistros or obstreperous pubs
on steep corners, deafening factory floors. For me
there was Rose Bay – I don't mean the school.
My authentic introduction was in company

of a retired widower cop who took our rent while we
shared his house and his ways …

*

It was Bill Cullen first taught me Australia:
grey slouch hat I shadowed along backyard tomato
jungles, on Cracker Night watching lights together,
amid cows and fridges at the Show, showbags,

the woodchoppers, and the jingling handful of old
RAS badges he bestowed on me, all I can touch
of him now. His gruff good humour, the methodical air,
mischief, dignity, sometimes a crustiness – as when

we'd mention him in Polish within earshot – a good man
I was fond of. But he died before the full fruits
of his easy teaching could reflect in a teacup
across a mutual Saturday table.

III

To what end these sounds and impressions?
I've allowed a few images to take hold, let them
worry and taunt recollection for what might clatter
out; permitted them to lead me, push me along.

And now they have pushed past a man of Australia,
man of the quiet land and level suburban lawns,

man of plain sense born of Dubbo and innocent
of irrelevant histories, though I am speaking loosely.

I mean the Old World histories, those from which Old
and New alike weave ever fresh histories of never
learning. For whatever the robust ethic or sunburnt
splendid illusion the centuries of Poland

belong as much to the playgrounds, sands and cottages
of diametrical vicinities, as much as Australia
springs from those crowded ages of zeal and
ramification, the continental epic.

Yet the people of the sands and cottages, lulled and
too many clinging, have learnt to muddle gratitude
with pride, scotch doubt with dull contentment,
reproof with sleep. Not for them the gentle challenge:

*

From a sun-drenched corner by the radio
you have listened to the world: no dead tyrants
of steel hammer or crooked cross are amix with your soil.

So you gave birth to no forbidden symbols,
carry no stinging scars underskin: at worst a blood
of forgotten twilights buried deep in your veins.

The empty cornucopia days you insulate
with papers that start backwards, bland in the face
of flickering clichés of pain.

Uttering silence, quietly you avert
your pale eyes from the darker eyes, the brooding eyes
of your hidden inland ...

*

I don't know what became of the listening boy,
the park-corner boy flying his first hectic bike,
speechless double expatriate curling shy marbles,
raw recruit who knew an old man.

I don't and I do: nothing really changes.
Next door they are burying Hitler.
I pencil ruminations on awkward pages lines
under my eyes. Cullen's house is long built over

and I have heard a procession of smashed leaders
banish perhaps a few complacencies. Maybe not.
When did we not ignore the telltale shudders
of history changing gears? So it merely shrugs,

uncoils more faiths and failures, triumphs, frenzied
orchestrations into common form – the endless flat
ongoing printed page, documentary evidence
just of continuity. Ancient design …

The myths and ideologies soon regroup, cluster,
collide on this crammed platform like gravid clouds
claiming a patch to pour into. But the inhabitants:
The Same. History keeps doing it to us … doesn't it?

*

And quietly you avert your pale, pale eyes,
uttering silence …

*

Poland is different now, a generation gulfs us.
From new corners I listen to the inexhaustible fifties.
I think of my mother, my father, I leaf the lost pages
of a hidden album lodged in secluded gardens

and though I understand little enough of the world
I think also of time, and time floats before me
like icing on waves ebbing back slowly to outline –
death. I begin to believe in time, the old swindler ...

I do and I don't,
for I am speaking loosely ...

Sentences

for Richard Appleton

I seem to recall
a quaint time I thought hitherto
said like concerto
    hithérto
and albeit to echo Arbeit
    álbeit

My friend who drank
red wine and wrote encyclopaedias
confessed he'd crossed
segments of youth
mouthing misled like wise-old
    mísled

The ostrich has drunk all the sand

Some thugs
I know up north pronounced a black
dream to kill a million
years of promiscuity
proclaimed this drunken chiliad
its tone a skull
its eye
the broken claws of a dead metaphor
crossed
on a field free of language

Between dreams
is where I thought all things
likely as death

Or as words
which I enunciated softly
rummed by the solo music of the alphabet
on a planet crammed with pages
and the burnt
ghosts of lexicographers who knew
surely
the impossibility of mispronouncing
 pain

Albeit hitherto misled
the ostrich is drinking still

From an Interview with a Faded Juggler

In those days she was lapsing rapidly
    Into liquidation. You see (and here
        The voice dropped) she'd make me fumble silly
           With impatience half the night, my fever

Rising crude within me, then she'd pipe
    The need for an *impératif* before the usual course
        So I'd splosh the glass again – she wiped
           It clean in one enormous gulp – and toss

The bottle, wait, until she'd done
    Sketching yesterday's fresh sign of early
        Menopause, so by the time we'd finally begun
           I'd feel the grim morning's surly

Tap on shoulder, but still squeezed the last drop
    Of night into the paling pillows, while
        My none too canny at best of times timing flopped
           Once more, and she'd destroy me with a smiled

Alas my love you do me wrong, to the tune
    Of the original. And my flushed quick try to link
        Wit with revenge by some keen countercoup soon
           Would evaporate absurd, would sink

Her merely to such lusty fits of silent piercing
    Laughter that it tore my blood adrift
        As day finally cracked the curtains, kissing
           Her black velour piano-seat with a grey mist

That always somehow scared me. So, as before,
    A vow: the last time, this. But listen: then
        It was the lastness of it moved me more!
           And I knew I'd be returning to her – maybe when

My funds ran low again, I rationalized.
   And so, despite succeeding daily wrestlings
      With myself, where gingerly I clean surprised
         The Id of me, started to glean caressings

Of a wisdom more autumnal, perhaps some clear
   Approach to purge the woman, I understood
      What no-one in his righter mind would know (here
         He cocked his face): she was rich food

For a glutton soul so frail and poorly travelled …
   Thus disexcused I'd hoist the phone and blithely start
      Afresh; and all that day I'd dream the sweet Devil,
         Greedy old whore after every man's heart

      And after mine after all.

Election Eve, with Cat

A tramstop swarms with schooligans, their brand
is chalked all over the matron's face.

Another busload tapers to the kerb
to take a breath. A briefcase with a watch

runs naked down the street, trips up the step.
The mob disperse, a well-cut

kindly teacher ponders past, he debates
the moralities of moving a snail.

The tramp is dozing richly on a bench
across the way, two schoolboys stand and perve

up at the sky. At fifteen on the brink of sex
a bookworm worries Tacitus

with teeth, tugs at her jeans, braces
herself for home. With the look of a man

ready to age the keeper of cigars and empty chairs
shops for spice on the wind, watches

a tramcar teeming like a Roman bus.
Somebody's wallet vanishes, a black convertible

with painted flames killed by a foolish dent
becalms itself. The traffic clings.

A blushing upstairs clerk scribbles a reply.
Tomorrow we condone another government.

Fugue

I *Sydney 1953*

Like a Chinese sniper on the 38th
I sit, I crouch askance, my frame fern-mottled,
    marking Foreman. I've watched him
from my window, licker of broad belts, stripe-saluter,
    the type to polish black boots

with his tongue – lovingly, oil
in his eyes. Not that he won't stand loud
    for his beliefs: Foreman's
the solid kind. Knows the rosy pollutions of our time,
    the wedges, well remembers

all war's lessons. Upper George saloons
audience him nightly, each sip extrudes fresh
    proclamations: how Chifley
would have sold us, how Ming should (metaphorically)
    be shot for playing plebiscites

to lose; how rhymeless the young's
new rhythms – undisciplined, uncouth. Oh, cultivated
    Foreman concedes himself; but pleads
only a sturdy shovel ever souped out true refinement.
    Admired De Groot on film,

claims to detest Hitler,
which is now the rage. When a routine disturbance
    materializes cops (deadly
control, clean chins, straps of intoxicating leather
    at the waist) Foreman blinks

excitement. Oh, the composure holds:
hands fumble imperceptibly, his breathing hangs.
    But I swear he foams
at the heart – the eyes soften, diffuse, hair-grease
    glistens a burning deference,

even his suit unrumples
as by magic; a smell of strength electrifies – now,
    I fancy, now could he choose to die,
tranced by one custody into the next ... Do I exaggerate?
    There are times surely when death

is a matter of some election. Well,
Foreman would gulp his measure, spill a last curse
    or a Parthian slit-eye snipe,
salute the bar, and swoop, glinting sergeant's buckle
    milkening his eye.

His drinkmates would pretend
    the setting sarcasm of his mouth was mad – would shrug,
resume the flow. I've watched them from my window
    and I know.

II *Dallas 1963*

Sunday fell away, the dead cusp of November.
Well, even the foreman sobbed, hulking no-quarter cruncher
with more than a twitch for the Russkies,
though his shop goes to his head sometimes and his knuckles
are pain.

Monday none of us could face the floor – anyway
the plant was shut. Over and over the unbelieving networks:
Zapruder's black motorcade, motion ...
catafalque. As if by catechism history might now deign
to alter.

The foreman was spotted by a couple of the guys
cutting his hair at Dino's, looking drawn. Tuesday missed,
Wednesday fronted up half stoned
and glassy-eyed, oddly unashamed to release his gut,
show age.

All week the stun of it – and those NBC frames
of a pistol thrust from camera-side, virtually Chicago.
Thursday himself again, an ugly mood:
spat nobody not half nuts could cop that fat barkeeper
Jew Ruby,

who'd reputedly done it to persuade the earth a Yid
has guts. You know it was the kikes not Commies had shifted
the First Catholic! Friday
he floored some fancy Polack welder over pool and Lincoln
Rockwell.

All week the channels belled the End of an Era,
only the drunker evangelists allowing any peace, any phoenix
could be seized from this
for symbol – but by the throat, the way the foreman pacified
stray pigeons.

III *Sinai 1973*

How reticent the dawn gathering the night behind
St Catherine, in this landscape that can only be chanted.
    There are skulls crypted here, centuries stacked
head to head, brooding who knows what destinies,

severed hopes, dispatchings; while we straddle our minutes,
our tank a stark statement against the crimsoning.
    Grotesquely, Formann seems to snore, one eye
half cocked, gun finger curled on a dulling buckle.

My cousins, he maunders under his beard, recall,
recall this wasted clump of grass was God's own ground,
    a flame from Jabal Mussa to ignite the world!
What voices lie extinguished in the silent mountain,

deaf now ... though a dozen Greek monks still drift the dim
quotidian rounds of this Potala. Formann's thoughts
    fold into mine, his mutter droning down,
down to a skeletal doze; now I can hear my blood,

trochaic, uninterrupted. Soon the trembling day
will trudge us out of this embankment. But O, Justinian!
    fourteen centuries – this is the shape of time:
no steeper church could astonish more completely

with how meagre our bones to bend history. We posture
in common at each other, dismal, across terrain
    impossible in its vividness. Groping in common,
how soon we reunite – the way the sand appeases

ancient marrow-shells. Commander Yuri Formann
is married a month; our waiting tank's a patient lover
    teetering on the breath of arousal. Another front
stretches round his bride. Gaza ... another dawn.

This bed of entrapment clamps about us all: crusading
Saracen, Pilgrim, Jew. In Cairo now ten thousand
    brides and mothers; my tribes due north cling
through another night. Tomorrow tank-rust; but today

our children tend a hate, it makes the desert bloom
both sides of Moses' crossing: scarlet spreading bloodrose,
    richly thorned, upearths another vein
of poison fruit. The mind becomes a cloister,

bell of an earthen flask that prisons comprehension, yet
breathes, conceives – burns, though the Bush is ash
    and dust tonight and mist three thousand years.
Yuri, look at me, wake! Tomorrow I'll be dead,

I know it in my spine. And you ... This monastery
will wait another thousand, twenty thousand more, while sands
    approach, ebb out, drift up, and heap, and blow:
there is no other place for them to go.

IV *Melbourne 1983*

Such natural death was uncharacteristic.
    We always thought he'd kick it throttled clean
by vodka in some terminal bigotry, the type
    they'd mug for fun,

with the pathetic droop when sober of a man
    guttering in his lack of consequence, futureless
but for the outburst imminent on drink.
    My father knew him

in the '50s – and whispered once he'd make
    a Blackshirt blush! Grim youth in Prague presumably
misspent, got through the war, wound up
    in Sydney '45,

altered his name, and worked. And drank.
    And raged against The Left. The bloodyminded union
Reds: line up along a wall or ship to Russia
    with the softer Libs

to savour paradise. Your Calwells, Whitlams,
    Hawkes: ambitious tools. Your one-eyed war protesters:
pawns of Marx. Your marching women, students:
    Kremlin-paid, else

drug-addicted bludgers on the dole ...
    Strange how this very man, dead, and scattered soon,
reflects the eye of a one-leg silent son, stooped
    on a crutch, remote;

from overseas somewhere (Mid-Eastern), bearded,
    pale for lack of sleep. Big, has brawn; air of a man
urgent to mourn concisely, cough, return
    to interrupted lives

elsewhere. Half-brother from the States –
    some dead-end Texas giant my father heard run down
by Foreman many times – of course he couldn't
    come. The rain,

compulsory at these rituals, scratches my cheek.
    Indifference is contempt, the way half-brothers get
when dim resentments of whatever birth put oceans
    up between them. Didn't leave

a roof, a will, a wish: nothing. A rusty box
    of locked and faded keepsakes, curious attachments
of a useless life, lingers somewhere unopened,
    orphaned, old. Perhaps

the only things he ever loved,
my father whispered once – he was intrigued in some
    mysterious way. This wind
will bring more rain. The swaying crematorium ferns
    dapple the day.

The Rearrangement

A garland for the times
To F.K.

I

Tomorrow I begin the Rearrangement of my books.
It should take me two days. Twelve hundred volumes
stand in the seven painted bookcases of oak
lining my square Chamber. These books have stood
the past year A to Z, in strict consecutive order
title by title, each one precisely in its place
in the perfect beautiful sequence. This year
I shall cluster them by Categories: of Prose,
Poetry, Music and Science, Art and Religion, Language,
Reference ... to Philosophy, History, even Travel.
Inside each field the books will be arranged
by Height, or Alphabet, or Colour – I'm not sure yet:
some years the undersystem doesn't quite emerge
till well beyond the Rearrangement.

II

The slow, relentless breathing of the night
enters my bookdream dusk. Former years parade,
old systems crowd: I see the Curving Edge (the height
discrepancy between adjacent books must not exceed
one millimetre, for a pleasing sweep); or
the Jagged Canyon (book-heights have to clash
undustably, like skylines); the Kaleidoscope (here
no neighbouring spine-hues of a kindred wash);
or Rainbows (the reverse, with gentle flows of tone
gained – it can play curious little tricks
with the Chamber's centre of gravity); but now and then
the colour systems cost – I had to double back once
for miscounting red! This year the Categories again:
tomorrow I begin the Rearrangement of my books.

III

I close the books, dissolve within the dark. Only
a pulse vigils the universe of paper, cardboard, ink;
my Categories spin me to morning ... I shall wisely
launch the Rearrangement by removing
x books from every shelf, these to be addressed
in preliminary groupings on the floor. As the rows
run empty the mounting Categories will race
to re-enrol: books will crisscross the room, the boards
will rise and drop. My work can thus proceed
progressively, like paint. One year, like a fool,
I first unloaded all the books onto the ground. God,
those locked-up tottering columns! – I had to start anew
backstacking all. This time no moment will be wasted:
it should take me two days, twelve hundred volumes.

IV

I recede, sense the brooding rhythm of the pages fade,
a sleep inhales me ... I can breathe two nights from now
the finished Rearrangement. Usually at that point
an immense and joyous calm, a serenity of soul comes down:
my eyes can glorify the crisp slopes of a bookscape
reinfused, living again. I lean back in my chair
behind my desk and drink of my design – this deep
correctness, this true *order* of Book I've come to fear
so few must know. Of course, when I was younger
these were days of needle doubts and pain; I'd be racked
by impulses to alter, start afresh. Sometimes I succumbed,
emerging sapped, confused. Until a discipline was struck
I'd struggle to stay sane – yes, even mootings of suicide
stand in the seven painted bookcases of oak.

V

In the thickening music they lean, softly
pulsate. I sound my harpsichord: it carves this room
of volumes on the wall with stinging textures. Daily
at nine and four my selftaught fingers roam
discreetly (learning yet) the sharp unpolished keys
that clutch a corner opposite my desk. I'd safely say
the period following a Rearrangement, as the clean
patterns print themselves, swim magically under my eye,
is when I win the sheerest joy from practising
more of my Mozart's miracle D Minor. (I know you
Wolfgang, you composed my books!) Of music nothing
else – the Fantasy contains all beauty, every truth.
I've been perfecting it for *them*: patiently listening,
lining my square Chamber these books have stood.

VI

The books murmur to the dim territory they guard
till morning intervenes. Each day from ten to twelve
the Dictionary: edging a volume of the *Shorter Oxford*
deftly on desk I open at random, read the page disturbed.
Soon as my finger stabs a word unknown, a meaning
incompletely sensed, I scan the definitions and the source,
inscribe them in my Comprehensive Lists. I copy clearly,
and precisely as the entry stands. My vocabulary of course
is excellent, yet words are always willing to be found:
the list-books now contain some twelve thousand and forty
copperplated heads. (This copying is tedious work, but
repetition teaches.) Every July I quiz myself closely;
Januaries to come I plan to relist all the words learnt
the past year, A to Z, in strict consecutive order.

VII

Truer than midnight a silence is droning
deeply within me when the Words are done. There
touches me by noon an hour of calm; I need to sit, absorb
the morning's labours looking out the wall. The apartment
vantages my storey on the street below: diurnal buzz
of cars, a versatility of trucks and fumes teem
in both directions. My meditation is by Counting – viz,
how many vehicles of a certain colour will proceed
under my window, or a certain make. When a bus rolls past
I clench to read the bold commercial slogans on its flank.
It preys on me (a peculiar dread) that I must never miss
deciphering a sign. Unlikely though: they're noisy, plain,
the buses never speed. After I've eaten I survey the books
title by title; each one precisely in its place.

VIII

Before too long the paper dawn will push ... Deeper
I climb, along the bittersweetness of tomorrow's birth.
By afternoon the Chamber will be madness, throbbing
about me like an open wound. There'll be no turn
to pause, reflect, to *love* the mobile books (unsorted,
stacked or leaning, stooped or prone, they will anticipate
their current destinies). No need for me, as on the
normal days, to monitor alignments, check the spines,
inspect for fraying corners or riffle through for spots;
no need for spirit-level tests for warpage (weather-
made) or breathing-space adjustments for expansion.
But in tomorrow's disassembled chaos a phoenix order
waits, maybe the truest yet, to leave my books disposed
in the perfect beautiful sequence this year ...

IX

Again the print appears to slide, pulsate ...
I could identify each breathing volume by its touch,
by its aroma when the pages fan. No two are alike.
Sometimes in the night I start up from my sofa to attack
an itch, a stain remembered from the midst of sleep
haunting my peace. Or, a festering blemish of an afternoon
will peer through chords, arpeggios that are always with me
and all at once I'll dive for my eraser, fall upon
the smudge; or jump to reassess a crease I felt
I had succeeded in dispelling. Some days I'll agonize
all morning on a newfound fleck, sparring with myself,
possessed. I'd even swear the *style* a book employs
is oddly related to the faults I find – one year (perhaps)
I shall cluster them by categories of prose.

X

Apparitions swim, subside to blackness, flicker
in the broken demilight. A carlamp spins the ceiling
sweeping before it my beloved Pictures: print,
two maps, four photographs, each frame exactly hung
one foot above a shelf. The print: the *Sins* of Bosch.
The maps: 1. World, Political (Mercator); 2. the British
Isles, with watercolour counties jigsawed in. The photos:
(a) one microchip, many times enlarged; (b) this
very room, wide-angle portrait from a handheld
Nikon; (c) cadastral shot of an undistinguished
Eastern Suburb, with my building seen; (d) the NASA world
from space. The globe intoxicates – from this vantage
all books are circled into One. History is then faith. And
Poetry: music. And Science: art. And Religion: language ...

XI

Wash gently over the spines that people the mosaic
forest, moonfriend: than you and your waking familiar,
loyal as books, I need no other. Once, I admit,
a student in a skirt and brown beret tallied irregular
visits. I'd circumnavigate her soul boiling poor
coffee in the kitchenette beyond; we'd chat in riddles
on indefinite matters, waiting. Until I led her
into my Chamber ... Her eyes ignited in a frenzy I'll
be haunted by – she flung herself, she rummaged, groped
with feelingless licked thumbs my precious pages, while
I quivered in horror, paralysed. 'Stop!' I screamed '*Stop!*'
at last. She froze, backed out, and left. Dull
philistine: in seven calls her tricky mouth attained no
reference to philosophy – history – even travel!

XII

As a cloud opens the moon I observe a dead sky.
Tomorrow my room will be reborn. The panic once again
waxing towards a Rearrangement I've found I can allay
with Marbles. Yes. It works like this: I take up seven,
all a different hue; from the room's centre I propel each
gem to kiss the base of every bookcase. Next, I run
a metre-ribbon up from every ball, its perpendicularity
plumbing a sample-core of spines. Then
I select that book the centre of whose spine is least
imperfectly aligned against the tape, record its name.
These seven books are scrutinized for specks, the alleys
reshot softly (click!) into a central cluster. I shall
use the taws this year to demarcate the Category fields:
inside each field the books will be arranged.

XIII

The shrivelling Chamber swells for a moment,
strains the bleak stockade. Today, eve of tomorrow, how
my panic leapt! I paced the floor, skin itching, eyes that
stung, trying to listen to the Chamber: but the high-
pitched pianissimo of a silence perpetually sung
stoked my oppression. Nothing consoled me, marbles, words
or music – my very Mozart slipped like dust
through sluggish fingers (who'd believe how long
my palms had begged his subtle universe!). I knew the room
was waiting for my Resolution, deeply premeditated
and prepared-for act that purifies and calms, the careful
wording finalized for weeks. So I sealed the vow. My head
is now more limpid to enlight the subroutines:
by height or alphabet or colour, I'm not sure yet.

XIV

I drift on the uneasy dusk. Thoughts inspect each other
as my Resolution settles on the blood. Every twelve months
the ritual's the same: kneel in the centre, elongate the
right arm horizontally palm-down, dubbing the cabinets
separately in turn. When the rotation is complete
I shut my eyes, pronounce three solemn times the text
of the Resolution; then occupy the window trembling
somewhat, drained. It's true there's also joy, expectancy
(the Resolution sets the score of volumes I intend
to read) but it's a battle to apply the pledge:
spent by the Rearrangement, loath so soon to disturb,
drugged by contemplation of the new design, I'm negligent –
and suddenly I'm planning for the next. On top of that,
some years the undersystem doesn't quite emerge ...

XV

But this year it is going to be different.
As always I've elected 20 books (several from Science,
10 from Lives and Art). This time I *will* dispatch
the titles picked. A little less attention to the spines,
the peccadillos, the pursuit of form; less needle
soul-searching over a system's flaws and fewer deaths
of heart. My reading must abandon quarantine –
I'm getting older, for at sixty-three one could expect
more volumes read than … Yet, each time I tell
myself I've struck the Ultimate Order, that the ancient
round of Rearrangements may be stilled, I grow nostalgic,
cold; locate a longing for an heir. I love the Chamber
like a child. D Minor is its face within my skull
till well beyond the Rearrangement.

XVI

But this year it *is* going to be different …
I drift on the uneasy dusk, thoughts inspect each other.
The shrivelling Chamber swells for a moment
as a cloud opens the moon: I observe a dead sky
wash gently over the spines that people the mosaic.
Apparitions swim, subside to blackness, flicker
again; the print appears to slide, pulsate;
before too long the paper dawn will push, deeper,
truer than midnight. A silence is droning,
the books murmur to the dim territory they guard
in the thickening music … They lean. Softly
I recede, sense the brooding rhythm of the pages fade.
I close, the books dissolve … Within the dark, only
the slow, relentless breathing of the night.

A Girl of Nagasaki
9 August 1945

I

The moon is a wet cork.
Rummage through your moonfresh morning dream
with no dark yearning
but preserve. Savour the clarity your rebirth frees.
The moon is Japanese.

II

This sun must be God.
My shadow stands frozen in the blizzard's beam
and daylight deafens.
I drink the black lightning of momentary trees,
the sun is on its knees.

III

The moon is a dry disc.
Listen to the scrapings of a sunspent gleam
along the road of ash.
Scratch with setting eyes the astronomy you feared.
The moon has disappeared.

IV

My soul is flapping
in the Nagasaki breeze I ran through yesterday:
a thousand years ago
my ancestors fly kites into the noon. I have
no need of these.

I listen, listen to the unforgetting moon.
The moon is Japanese.

The Death of the Word
Berlin, Good Friday 1933

Never having acquired a taste for tragedy
you laughed. Last & loud
were the eulogies, inaudible
the smooth descent of the casket cranked by 4
diaphanous monks munching nonchalant
leaf growing graveside. Spitting
gouts of wet weather shielded my tears &
rumours of thunder scattered the onlookers.
The coffin rested on planks 1830
millimetres under & the snivelling parson
laid the first sod lightly & limping
so as not to soil
a reputation for spiritual detachment. You
continued laughing under your teeth, chattering
& cold the spectators floated off & I stood
for no further ceremony short of
patience & pocketless of coin to bury
the last of these exorbitant rites, received
only the blank & slow sufficiency of 2
thug-eyed slabs of man
come to deposit a stone bearing a cryptic
epitaph: *Anagram is an anagram
of Anagram.*
        And you laughed, unencumbered,
never having acquired a knack for comedy.

Narrowing of the Arteries

It is remembering the names of kings
their dates   the odd assorted thumbnail
deed   Spending a ten-day
vacation from the music counter
to count köchel into memory   Annotating
the complete complex prosodies of
a friend   Teaching a computer
the weight of your fingers   It's occasionally
squatting in unmade beds   bodies
of strangers   restaurants distinctly short
on sawdust   And sometimes
the first day of season quite unnoticed
or unseen flicking the poems of karol wojtyła
under the rose at the window
seat   Somewhat catholic   jewish   it is never
as simple as it sounds   carries a sense
of ribbonry   the split of hairs   a quizzing
after knowledge   Ambushed
by longings largely invited it lowers
its book a moment   It's the inquisition
showering itself   an imploding
orgasm way ahead of a desire
to whisper anything   anything   I
would say it is unmistakably a phenomenon
of the city   the land is too liquid
too longsighted   extends no shrift to suburban
theosophies   Sprawl's all very well
but

Arrival

Approaching the capital you unfurl the map.
An entropy closes, the land hands over quietly
And tapering highways thrust into this vestibule
        Of incipient city,
Accept a film of thickening urbia, begin to ache under
The pied strata, illuminations of nail, rust and
        Splinters. I remember

The dive into new dangers. Obstacles sprout
At countless crossings: every machine's lewd rictus
Grills me with sarcasm, sun-dazed lamps blankly stare
        Themselves into barrels
Of numb snipers who wait frozen in midday nearness.
Abruptly it occurs to me that memory's the one
        Thing we truly possess,

And I shed all but the lean of these silences –
Plazas exposed, towers that could so easily tumble
Now, tomorrow, earths that yet must yawn to defy
        Mere architecture.
Even park patches gleam with a brittle attentiveness,
Grassy knolls abound. There is nowhere to hide in this
        Town of hiding places.

But on the nineteenth level of another Travelodge
I flicker weakly the mint Gideon, pronounce at random.
Darkness suspends itself, town is a distance, a
        Dull twitching of neon
Deep under the drowned ambiguity of night. Somewhere
A book on a long-ago shelf snaps into place with a thud
        Of dust or nostalgia.

Is it some god addressing a jolt in my blood
Or a mundaner longing? I've been likely in recent years
To transfix an idol in a glossy Roman edition, or
                Smatter among Proverbs;
Last month I cried in a synagogue, stupidly, struck cold
By a choir. Suddenly impatience – I recall this inn
                Is of the suburbs' world:

Tomorrow the centrum; no claims on the past, all
The dogs have been put to sleep. Yet the quiet eye
In the mirror's abroad with its customary reports.
                Let them lie. Let them lie.
The universe runs down, without a splinter of pity …
What place is this? You begin to unfurl the map
                Approaching the city.

from *Sleeve Notes*

(1992)

Sisyphus

I choose my boulders carefully,
They are scattered like words across the white plain;
I scoop my syntax from the clouds' dictionary –
The path to wisdom is difficult, rich and mundane.
I have my nostalgia, the soft exquisite aching
That lulls and lacerates; and I can dream
The dazzling city that drives upward to the horizon
Beyond the land where the rumbling boulders lean.
One evening soon, as the crescent overtakes me,
I'll slip discreetly over the edge of the plain
And into the valley beyond, because I know
The song of terrible grace that summons me.
But the clouds are backing away; an exquisite pain
Is pleading for me to stay. How can I go?

What Matters

The old roof creaking in the rain
A moth fussing about under the light
A mug of gold steam on a windy night
The impermanence of tunnels, a line of type
And the face inspecting itself
Like a stranger, bitterness
When it slants across the blade of the years
Love of course
Uninvited tears, a letter
From a faraway friend long thought lapsed
The stars in a child's eyes
The trust in its hand, music, sharp apples
The rent, a miniature wooden box given
As a memento, in which nothing is kept
Paper, wine, the möbius mystery of sex
Flaws forgiven yourself, a good bed slept
In, several books waiting patiently
Twenty years, a pen quietly leaking
Old pain, the old fears creaking

The Old Song

for Mal Morgan

He wrestles the wind like a skater
    struggling uphill
Umbrella bent she swims against the rain
My daughter rushes in with some new excitement
A spiritual virgin somewhere hits the hay

The seagulls rotate like a windmill
    in the tropics
They re-enact a song as old as Babel
An opera-star whose mediocrity is staggering
Begins to comb his Gideons for a label

Dreaming of claret and the clotting
    of his sickness
The lion consumes his morning-after hock
An architect of spears surrenders all his Gothic
His grounds become the flimsiest on the block

My son rushes in with a biscuit
    in a bottle
And a photo of a twirling parade
The demagogue refocuses his single-lens reflex
A print is more impressive framed

We box in the rain like forgotten
    olympians
Futile as midsummer skaters
At night we re-invent the same stuttering songman
Or hit the sack, full of coal and potatoes

German China
In Time of Peace

Berlin by night. The boys and girls are dancing
On the wall, the nations gape.
    From across the Rhine
The numerologists are busy necromancing
Numbers like 56 and 61 and 68,
    It's 1989.

That international combustion engine known
As history stalls, restarts with a kick
    As the tanks trundle:
Back east and westward, skirting the old bone
Of the Brandenburg, skirting the brick
    Where clichés now crumble.

They say the waters are breaking, on the battlefield
The waters are parting. No flowing prophet to fetch
    The children across
But they come, the tide of Europe stands back like a shield
On each side. Satellites and silos twitch,
    Argue the toss.

No flowing prophet – just this conjuring messiah,
This magician: yesterday's joke was Czech
    Tanks in Red Square;
Today we fancy Soviet treads amid the spires
Of Bucharest. Remembering June we retrace his steps,
    Gulping for air.

While after three thousand Passovers the windy sage
Of London turns, his German gaze locked on another gate,
    Another wall:
Greater and grander, older, buckled by blood and age,
Twisting into a redder sea – a flood made
    In his name, a Fall.

The chariots of the commissars crossed with a zeal
Blameless of prophecy, achieved in the Celestial Square
    A pyramid of death.
Onward they race, westward towards that dancing wheel
Of triumph, the midnight tango's commandment. There
    The backs are turned.

The tall blindfolded virgin with her Scales
Betrays a smirk out of the corner of her mouth,
    Slouches like a scribe –
Closer inspection reveals her faded jeans, but fails
To locate the face – she's lost in the crowd,
    They suck her inside.

They're strolling along the wall, that other one;
The Square, the other one, has emptied
    And the guns are gone.
A documentary crew clipping some anniversary has come
To claim the freezing dawn, pre-empted
    Only by the moon. Stoic, alone.

On the Theology of Ants

Picture an insect
circling a lifetime
in a covered jar. Secure the jar
inside a canvas bag stuffed with
faded clothing, rags and torn stockings.
Enclose this in a suitcase full of books
and old journals, sealed, strapped and slotted
in the back of a rusting station wagon
locked in a cluttered shed. Now imagine
that the garage is appended to a cottage
strung to a tree within a sprawling suburb
whose proximity to the city is ambiguous.
Elevate your vantage to locate the black towers
puncturing clouds that suspend them in space. Go
higher, higher, to incorporate the spill
of a massed metropolis, and then its edges
fringing the urban dusk and blending fast
with fields and pastures, plains and rolling earth.
A moment, and you stack
the crisscrossed chiaroscuro geometric grid
slanting, sliding north – and to the south, and west,
and east into the sea. Then the horizon and the end
of earth: receding, fading, darkening,
unreal – perspectives vanish, and
the thud of black.

The imprisoned ant,
still circling, nearly dead,
has spent his life devising metaphysics.
He has thought out the nature of the universe,
the origins of matter, the designs of time.
Serene and certain, he loves the calm of knowledge,
prepares glowingly to confront his Maker:

Whom most of his kind believe to be sixlegged
but his own rarer perception, its divining spirit,
already can sense more correctly ...

After a Meeting of the Mahler Society, Melbourne, 1952

for Walter Adamson

Watching the children, he observes
the overwhelming sanity of children.
At last he has learnt not to be noticed,
he has become Australian – he recalls
the canals, the golden-brown September afternoons,
the music-room at –
'Music is a higher revelation than philosophy,'
Beethoven said. Mahler, triple-exile,
wanted to swallow the whole world
in his symphonies: he at least was spared
the death of Europe – even if his continent
was about to perish on the *spiaggia*
with Aschenbach. But the canals,
the glass, and oh, the cantos – in the German,
the Italian style. How in the world
could the twentieth century collogue with
1300? History. Had he not turned
with breathless devotion the textured pages
of his father's *Welt-Atlas*
seeking out Venice, the Red Sea, Sydney?
He knew that all those colours had their meaning
yet they made him so strangely sad.
So he'd turn instead to his dog-eared schoolbooks
for the answers, but they didn't know:
Ich weiss nicht, was soll es bedeuten,
sang the maps, mysterious with longing.

Quadrilateral
A journey

I *Sea Vision*

Recurring dream: I stand
on the edge of an enormous ocean. The sea, vexing
the sand, is suddenly driven

to a boiling stillness, flexing
it seems the black depths of its intentions
into a will, and then – collapses!

Now the terrible declensions
of a bizarre new grammar are about to be revealed.
The sky mentions thunder,

but the elements must steel
for the greater nightmare slowly, rapidly unfolding.
I feel a nausea rifle my senses –

end is what my sockets are recording!
I want to rush, regurgitate my terror blindly,
but the body is dammed

by fear. For, all around me
the stretched horizon-lines of ocean are receding,
shrinking out to sea,

the churning brine is feeding
back upon itself, crumpling, crazily falling –
the very waves have turned:

something is recalling
a billion years of mystery back into primal air.
(Crawling or prone, writhing,

the creatures of the sea prepare
a doom: the sand, unceremonious, will suck them
bare, soon the features

of a longing never stemmed
but in the dimmest plasma dreams will reunite,
bent to an ancient song ...)

So, peeling back now as if ignited,
ocean is vanishing: the fast unfurling bed –
blighted, grotesque and cracked,

craggy, segmented –
is waxing, darkening in a monstrous extension
bled of design, the steady

dropping of an endless canyon
into roaring incessant space ... At last, at last,
a bottomless, unstopping

smouldering moonscape past
all thought of sea is spread into the distance.
I gasp, clutch at the concept

but meet a horrible resistance.
Thought must end here: the skull of history glowers,
the vista waits, complete

with weird and dripping towers,
cliffs that clamber past the grope of what was vision.
My powers fail, I yield –

how can such collision
with infinity be met? Blood no longer bursting,
decision dead, I stand

on the edge, thirsting
no longer for a bygone sea: my will beyond my saving,
I nurse the wedge

at work already in the paving
that is memory ... Soon we shall all forget the ocean,
graving our stubborn earth,

our ghettos, with a stranger notion:
We are the people of the rock – that is our message.
Our portion is to fornicate with shadows ...

You'll shed no brackish pity for our passage.

II *The Rock*

'Ladies and gentlemen, welcome to the Rock.
The age of this monolith is impossible
to decide, but primitive observations of
planetary behaviour are known to have been made
from the summit some forty thousand years ago.
The ancient superstitions once revered the Rock
as "Birthplace of the Gods", a colossal mountain
capped by perpetual cloud. Indeed, at least four

 'separate traditions still incorporate
this locality in legends of the founding
of their faiths and ministries. The more romantic
in temper talk of the Rock as the petrified
heart of a Titan of protohistory, or
the fabled landing-plateau of a grim vessel
that drifted for centuries (and here the scriptures
oddly coincide) before the dying remnants

'of the race, a man and woman variously
denoted, needed each other again. The less
oblique of mind subscribe to tales of a giant
meteor whose shattering descent demanded
implantation. Some even maintain that the stone
once guarded the gates of a great ocean; others
that it envelops the final repository
of mythical kings, riddled with tunnels and mazed

'by strange interior tombs and treasure-chambers.
Certain cults believe that once every millennium
a foundling may venture to address the Rockface,
the reply a conundrum whose key will unlock
a lifetime of perfect wisdom – or deliver
death, instant but cruel. Perhaps in this connection
it is sometimes said that dark, unspeakable deeds
were enacted in the bowels of the monument,

'which is then defined as a wicked and most
ingenious network of diabolical cells,
a honeycomb of torture-chambers, or a dim
vault where astonishing implements of murder
on scales now undreamt-of were devised. Even so,
some prefer to regard the Rock as the solid
manifestation of Will, the essence of Time;
but this is doubtful ... Thank you for your attention.'

III *From the Air*

Well, Mercury's ascending,
the twins seem warm and vaguely settled;
can't for the life of them spot the worm within the apple.

Oh, the sky is full of whispers,
they stroll the ruins of a mighty garden;
ancient and stooped they feel an exquisite nostalgia harden,

Well, into a hymn: *What*
could have been better than this magic wood?
They turn: *Life will be just as better, if not good.*

Oh, what a monument they build,
what a globe, with its four great fortresses;
stoic servants and samurai, stern scholars and sorcerers.

Well, presently the sphere
is bloodying its axis (the warriors accrue):
We shall die (they scream) *if it's the first thing we do!*

Oh, no; live, and recant!
(re-echo the conjurors, huddled in song)
Or rue for the rest of your lives, if you live that long.

Well, slowly our twinlings,
much travelled by now, join the general fun:
What the hell! A little bit of pain never hurt anyone –

Oh, and all that knowledge
to plunder, pray to … No nation is rational,
and at least *their* outlook now is thoroughly international.

Well, at this point
the clouds' patience finally elapses.
The twins, still experimenting, are way out of practice.

Oh, the mercury is rising
and Gemini find fire too seductive …
Voice: *I don't mind praise, so long as it's constructive.*

IV *Trial by Fire*

So, the treachery of words,
and we are left to our devices after all.
We seem to have travelled a lifetime, you and I,
in search of the transmuting flame, feeding
off the warmth of each other's fear. And now we reach
an evening of rain pounding in the gables, the cool
jacaranda dripping its regal blood once more. Soon
I shall sweep the blossoms from the path outside –
someone may still wish to walk it ...

We spun histories to one another
while the universe, defenceless, continued to strain
in its bearings; we made out inventories of doom,
squinting out of our private little infernos;
we watched oceans break over the world, draw back
to expose a charred decay. Yet we clung to our measure
of safety because we possessed each other.
And even on an evening such as this, when sex
seems foolish and the intricacy of your breath
on a sleeping pillow merges with summers in a garden
behind a house on a street within the capital
of a land I have long since forfeited,
my ego aches for reassurance and the old alchemy
persists with its demands.

How often we have studied the inscriptions
on passing faces, how clearly we thought we knew
the pain of stone at a city gate. Remember
the day you declared, half dreaming, that a boulder
we nestled like lizards in the sun
was listening, absorbing the rays of our geometry?
I laughed of course, yet when we pressed our ears
into the grain, I swear I heard the murmurings of gods,
agony of martyrs, the joy of a butterfly
forty centuries fossil ... But never spoke.

Strangely inspired, you clambered,
leapt from the pinnacle like some heroine of Greece.
That night we bickered on the afterlife:
I mocked your certainties – what betrayal!

So, the treachery of words, this alone is left us.
We've debated eternity time and again
in the dialects labelled Religion,
translated atheism (the most passionate theology),
circled our own unspoken fire,
to arrive, in the end, at – this:

We, our roots pounded and torn
    by the surge of a cataclysm worthy of legend ...
We, our generations tapering behind us,
    victims of a treachery beyond words ...
We, who inherited an epoch without time,
    a history stripped of its possessions ...
We, who incurred the terror-mask of Janus: behind us
    the burning, ahead the flame – a passion
    so fervent it was etched in catechisms; so cold
    we sickened daily at the sight of steel ...

    who, like our parents
    confronted finally with themselves, could
    only whisper: *Can I believe? After all this, can I
    have faith?* ...

We return.
The treachery of language leads us back
like shadows to a torch. The dead alone have been
transmuted. And while we ponder
whether the dead we praise, malign, may listen
to our hearts; while we plot the survival of words,
plan beyond catastrophes more terrible than death,
we discover we can still compass love,
least treacherous of the human declensions.

The ocean too returns for the tide, the rock
will perch forever on its earth. Between the howl of space
and the crawling lava we survive our living
somehow. The jacaranda's full of feathers,
your breath is constant and the month is waxing. Soon
the plotting horizons will devise another dawn ...

Hold me. We will yet cheat the elements.

A Lecture in the Public Library

She turns obliquely in her seat
her finger gleams
and as they meet
his eye jumps to where the jumper meets
the jeans

Their lines discreetly intersect
circle and tangent
and they effect
a congruence whose chosen side-effects
are urgent

But in the privacy of dawn the unkind
pyramid appears
he knows the sign
his head explodes with all the intricate designs
and fears

He turns: her trousers hang inverted by
the unmade bed
and in the sly
kitchen quietly she posts a double slice
of bread

They break their toast and strain their tea
much as one might
while in the entropy
of six oclock his car and his trapeze
await

And as he parallels the empty kerb
she locks her room and
showers for the third
time thinking We're all so ridiculously
human

The Face in the Flower

A man stands by a shivering fire
in the cool refectory of a disused inn
within a kilometre of a half-demolished city
during a pointless critical war.
He is smiling to himself
the smile of a maddening tyrant or a
middle-aged drinkwaiter coming to terms with kitsch.
His hands polish a bubble of brandy
whose rim is dusty and warrants only the dullest
reflection before his eye wanders
to the portrait of the most beautiful woman
in the province hanging above the fireplace.
She sits in an ornate vestibule-chair
wearing a benevolent cream-coloured robe
through which her flowing outlines are discerned
and in her black-nailed hand she clutches
a regretful flower with the face
of a demented infant. There is probably a tear
snaking down her cheekbone
but the lamp that would illuminate
the portrait is dead
so it is impossible to guess the true domain
of her expression. But clearly she is
beautiful in the sad half-light and the face
creasing the flower has the quiet menace of envy
for it is far from beautiful.
It challenges the man to a contest
he has already lost
while with its open petal hand
it gropes impatiently for the vulva the breast
the lips of the girl in the translucent gown

whose slender black-nailed grip
on the floundering boy-flower
weakens as he watches
and downs briskly his last burning lacrimosa
before smashing the innocent glass
against the vanishing fireplace pediment.

Also Silence

for Lex McAulay

The urbanity of language unburdens us.
Dawn. A battlefield's leavings.
List them:
the turf gashed as if by a giant bumbling contraption,
a lagoon of cold puppets
spilt at random or fixed in the freeze of a shutter,
rubbertrees smashed with the brute velocity
of fear, duty, the grand designs of a faith;
handguns, torn patches of thought, the odd limb
bent or prepared to topple
in the high grass tramped by the lumbering of dice;
a sheet fluttering in the flex of the sun;
also silence.

In the midst of it all he rolls the revolving door
like a hoop into the lobby,
clears the receptionist
with an old affirmative salute and swims past
the assembled hardware of the exam room.
The department. Palms in pots,
inkwells of the old school now pencil porcupines,
the *officiers* aligned pecking round the room,
some gazing at cups, all tie-impaled.
Striped. Diagonally with red. Or blue.
In the director's office are files of statistics.

All right. She's not your world's
most exhilarating secretary – none of that
lapleaping nylon middle-America
snagged on corners of executive blottingpads,
and scarcely ever a smudge
of the high life under the lash of a morning;
but you know where you stand, the value. She types

with the speed of a silver bullet in the back,
takes a vicious dictation,
and her shorthand would pacify the last martinet.
Unmarried, noncommissioned, she couldn't have a lovelife
(could she?)
epitomizing as she does every absence of charms
charmers hold in contempt. Nevertheless –
he thinks he loves her. She enjoys his voice,
listens with compassion to the toughest combats
(doesn't she?).

Their children play with gocarts, tommyguns;
he finds vindictive satisfactions
in the morning print. He reads till ten,
changes his job, freelances
for an airbrake manufacturer dabbling in transmissions
on the side. They begin to rattle one another,
long ago wearied of his need to explain,
her imagineless
indifferent capacity to please.
The twins leave, the baby adopts drugconcerts
and sick friends with alarming hair;
she moves in with a divorced promoter
to miscarry. The twins offer something
at the doormat. Not for long.

He changes jobs again, moves north
but finds the hayfever playing up. Returns,
they take up bridge.
Between alternate Thursday nights he shuffles labels
in the pricing department of a wholesale hardware merchant,
midnights attempts the cryptic
or the wife.
Sometimes he meets her with an open hand.
She slips out one evening never to return. He laughs
at the pathetic clichés in the note
then crumples like a Charlie in the wet.

The urbanity of language unburdens us.
The turns, the errors, violences, the lusts,
the smallnesses solidify into a molten core
then harden; in the convalescent home
he pares the loving detail from the rock
like an oldtime dad peeling infinite apples,
the leavings gleaned
are like a delicate skin lifting out forever
from its fist of flesh – and dropping ...
dropping random strands to the wheelchair floor.
List them:

The stinging childhood, call of an olive camaraderie,
combat, a madness in the rubbergrove,
precision of the wound,
the glimpse of death, exhilaration of Truth's solo moment;
then the retelling ...
And beyond, a mystery: shuffling throat, a curse,
a trend to viler gestures, and the sense
of hidden quagmires rife with injury.
The soiled midnights now, the mealtimes left untouched,
and music from a speaker by the bed.
Also silence.

The Golden Age

She squats dozing a bit
beside the sleeping quickly child,
traces a dialectic old as breath
between them now. It frightens her, somehow.

She floats a limpid finger
to the sill: the ants withdraw
looking guilty. Exorbitant flowers
spatter the vase across from the door. What for?

Outside, the buses blunder
to a stop. She lifts her bulk,
tests a bathroom looking-glass account
of gibbous coming silhouette. No, not yet.

Zero to five –
the golden age. She goes inside
the hurting slowly skull. She
peers at her son in alarm: was it a cry? Why?

She stands unclenching
her spine. The infant vaguely
stirs. A half-eye maybe opens warm
in its trance. The dust-motes, aerobatic, dance.

Ambit

The old white spider
    crawls through my hair as I sleep
and when I walk he waits to survey his work.
    I twiddle a dial, I adjust a belt, or a cork,
and crouch again to my glassbeadgame, or I weep,
    and he waits like a glittering hawk.

The old white spider
    has devised an astute coalition
with the letter, the syllable, the word, and the endless line.
    I shake out the pages to ascertain his position
but the web on the wall isn't his, it is mine,
    and he waits like a statistician.

The spiderweb mesh
    is a mirror with roads and canals,
like a focusing lens I go in and I go beyond it;
    time disappears, the illusion of movement dispels
to uncover the key to the gate that can never be opened,
    and he waits like a film and learns.

The old white spider
    ensnares me again and again
and the only escape is the spiderweb notchings of time,
    and the stepped horizon the one possible climb,
and the sole consolation: my city of runes, the zen
    of a master entangled in slime

who waits like a fly for the end.

Fragment

These tunnels I have snapped shut behind me
    of semblances and their delicate committees
    of inland waterways that flow nowhere
    of lava, crimson but frozen to the touch
    of that ceaseless acupuncture recollection
        (but not nostalgia)
    of beggars and the painted goddesses
    of the tinkling cowbells of remorse
        (but not compassion)
    of the cool denuded paddocks sloping into sleep
    of the vertical and endless
    of the pinched multitudes with their prayer-ratchets
    of time
        (but not necessarily of clocks and lithographs)
        (no not of the world)
        (not yet)
And certainly not of music and the ocean
    the heartbeat-breath and the measuring of words
    the cold glare of dispassionate marble
        (that understands all)
    the mirror into which all must disappear
    the other glass that spins, ever advancing
        (that has seen everything)
        (everything there is)
    the truism of cubes that contain bone
    the truth of things, things
    the insanity of wind in a blinded poplar
    the immensity of all that must not be said
        (yet must be)
And not the step of a woman on threadbare carpets
    down four dozen centuries
    and the pain she deposits as she walks
    the pain of the objective stars
    burnt out before they can flare into a death

        all the pain of crossbars and a shield
        receding like a printer's dot design
        to reveal the face that reveals nothing
        but a distance, and history closing its pores
And surely not
        the paradox of love
        the meniscus that trembles in a flickering cup
        the sudden truth of water on parchment
        the scrawl of ink's silences
        and this
Why else look back to repossess the choice
        the padlocks impervious to all implements
        the latches rusting nicely in their longitudes
        the heave of doorways immovable as age
        the must of sealed tunnels that are memory
Why else
        this impotent pernickety finesse
        this fumbling for a key encased in rock
        this solitude of tunnels in the sand
        these tunnels I have snapped shut behind me

Elgar Revisits Worcestershire, 1984

Edward Elgar was born in a cottage at Broadheath, near Worcester, in 1857.
Fifty years after his death the cottage, now a national treasure, was visited by a ghost.

How painful they can never truly know
Me in this world. Music deceives,
Can cover up the music it contains – go
To Vienna, study Mozart's last immortal scores,
Beethoven's late inscriptions. How it grieves
Me to be standing by the side
Of this sententious expert on the Variations,
Who's never stepped *into* the notes they hide,
Never peeled back his sticky annotations
To *listen* to my ink. How readily he breathes
His reverence, rolls a voice
Dipped in a second-hand sea. His lazy choice
Of worship's not *my* life, it leaves
Me desolate for a life I know ...

    When music was a secret pocket plugged
With bread and cheese for lanes I cycled on;
    When music was my secret garden dug
High above music-shops long since shuttered, gone;
    When music was the leaves I leant against
Limping into the wind; the secret snow
    When music covered the recumbent glades
Of passion, and the earth's mysterious song.

Most painful they can never truly know
My music's dark communion – not with God
(The giver and creator), nor the fleeting Self,
But with another music's more mysterious hold:
The stealing of the enigmatic earth
Within my heart. There they can never go,

Nor I ever return.
              But here amid my leavings, we can mourn.

A Life

I *Entropy*

Into the web he spins wider and wider
measuring tenderly every strand.
The slightest movement panics the spider,

can send him scattering, or bring him beside
a tangled victim his body will bend
into. The web he spins wider and wider,

beyond the core. A confused outsider,
for instance, straying, alert to withstand
the slightest movement, panics; the spider

prepares to pounce upon her, guide her
back to the heart, into his hand,
into the web he spins ... Wider and wider

he circles daily, deafer, blinder,
the circle condensing – until in the end
the slightest movement panics. The spider

ponders. The spider is striving to understand.
The slightest movement panics the spider
into the web he spins wider and wider.

II *A life*

And as the dawn unnoticed crept
along the passageway, I gingerly descended
the rungs of memory until they froze
into my sleep. I softly slept

the entire morning away, rose
around eleven and stealthy as any bandit
(and as the dawn) unnoticed crept

thief-like the creaking upstairs floor to those
ridiculous banisters I'd so often blended
into. My sleep I softly slept

all over again while the soul chose
in a trance a dream discreet as the dusk is candid
(and as the dawn unnoticed); crept

unconvincingly, and clumsily I suppose,
into that reverie; and from there – having bent it
in to my sleep – I softly slept

another hour, several more, awaking close
to midnight, dozing off. The night-time ended;
and as the dawn, unnoticed, crept
into my sleep, I softly slept …

III *The moth*

There is a knowledge indistinctly heard
Behind all that I know and all I am.
Behind the turning socket of the world

It coruscates like some shade harmony, stirred
In the pedalpoint of sleep: I understand
There is a knowledge. Indistinctly heard

And brief, it splashes into colour, flag unfurled
To sputter in the wind – a wind whose chant
Behind the turning socket of the world

Can barely reach me. Yet the droning whirl
Of mind and circumstance, and entropy, demand
There is a knowledge, indistinctly heard

But true. And I'm committed, I am spider-held
To circumnavigate its soft command
Behind the turning socket of the world.

And as I write these lines, my syllables meld,
The music haunts the shadow of my hand.
There *is* a knowledge, indistinctly heard,
Behind the turning socket of the world.

Sleeve Notes

I *Clavier*

He sits at a table next to an instrument,
a pale plain face, betrays no flush
of creative fever or concentration.
A candlestick, solitary, scatters light,
the eyes are shining – otherwise darkness.
He seems to be jotting something down
or he could be sketching: there is much paper,
and over it flutters a hand with a slender
wrist but the strokes of a master conductor.

And it must be late for the night is silent
behind a window shivering faintly
stained by a curtain half lit by shadows
cut by the lamp on the cluttered table.
It's true that he could be correcting a notebook
or dotting a journal, yet something implies
a darker performance to be in progress:
maybe he's pouring his life in a letter
or splashing confessions onto a page …

But wait! The face, with its flesh and stubble,
a tremor touching the line of the mouth,
the lips intense, the trousers vaguely
dappled and lost in the dredge of the floor …
And could he be humming? A breeze has entered
to slide like a cat on the open keyboard,
and if it riffles the lay of the almanac
spread on the table, the merest flicker
will probably do to betray the season:

January 1791.

II *Clarinet*

Clearminded morning
Fresh, concentric
I sink gently into the mystery
Cradle myself in music

Gestures of the soul
Fleeting, eternal
They prod delicately beyond meanings
Impossible longings
Merge, converse in silhouette
While thought is defied to entrap them

Suspended moment

Somewhere half across the world
a desire formed and froze
a skylark hovered remembering something
a little boy's heart swelled with ecstasy
while a teardrop poised on a miraculous leaf
mirrored his wonder as he watched it
inhaling the sun

And the world is flooded with music
And I can cry

III *Rezitativ*

To the Municipal Councillors of Vienna

Sirs! In the period of Herr Kapellmeister
Hofmann's illness I contemplated
taking the liberty to apply for his post,
hoping (my musical talents, achievements
being known abroad, my name being held
in high estimation everywhere
and I myself having several years
enjoyed the honour of the appointment
of Court Composer here in the capital)
that I might not be deemed unworthy
of this position, and the consideration
of your highly learned corporation.

Kapellmeister Hofmann regained, however,
his health, and under these circumstances
(for with all of my heart, may his life be long)
I had the thought that it might possibly
be of some service to the Cathedral,
and to you, Sirs, if I were appointed
assistant to the aging Herr Kapellmeister
– without a stipend for the time being –
thereby deriving the opportunity
to help this venerable man in his office
and also securing the approbation
of your most learned corporation

By the performance of various duties
to which I think that I quite justly
may deem myself most peculiarly fitted
through my acquirements in ecclesiastical
and secular styles of music.

IV *Obbligato*

To Choirmaster Stoll, Vienna

Please find for my wife a small apartment,
she needs two rooms, or one with a closet
(but on the ground floor); the ones I favour
are those at the butcher's where Goldhahn was, if
they're available …

Or try to find something close to the waters
(but on the ground floor). My wife's arrival
will be on Saturday, Monday the latest.
The ones at the notary's place'll be fine, though
the butcher's are best …

V *Basso ostinato*

The Count Zeccucelli is the ultimate bore.
Last night at the Rechbergs' he started to tell us
Of his amorous exploits in Florence and Venice
And in the *campagna*. He plainly embarrassed
Our mistress, who nibbled as never before.

He opened by noting that Austrian ladies
Are colder and harder, too sober, too firm and
Too pious (I swear it!); he settled this sermon,
'A *Mädchen* is neuter gender in German!'
And noted how willing a Tuscany maid is.

Then he proceeded to catalogue random
Encounters with servants (the 'chambergirl game'):
When a maidlet in London enkindled his flame,
'Like Caesar I saw her, I conquered, I came!' –
The old Don himself would have blushed over that one.

There followed an episode hinged on a virgin
Renowned for her virtue, who stopped where she stood
And replied 'Goodness me!' when he spotted her rude
In the river one day – 'So I goodnessed her good!'
One shudders the bellies he must have made burgeon.

The master concluded the lesson with more of his
Thoughts on the alphabet. Item: the vowels
Are 'the womb of a language, the space that allows
Procreation of meaning, the time that endows
That meaning with life, like the feminine orifice'.

But claiming the hard philological core
Are the consonants: 'Phallic, priapic, it's they
That *elevate* lust to the Devil's domain'!
Well, if Hell is a hole in Heaven, both I
And old Newton have more than an apple to answer for …

(My own favourite letter is K.)

VI *Aria*

To Constanze, Baden

… Take care not to slip in the bath
and never go about by yourself.
If I were you I'd skip the odd day
lest the treatment should sap your strength.

I hope somebody spent the night-time
near you. Believe me, what I wouldn't offer
to be with you now in Baden! To fight my
boredom I composed for my opera

another aria. I was up before five. It
may amaze you: I've got my watch
back, but couldn't rewind it
alas, for lacking the key to match —

is that not sad?
Schumbla! Now there's a word to ponder!
I wound the big clock instead ...
A thousand kisses I send you, dear one. *Adieu.*

VII *Flute*

Three knocks announce a terrible serpent
Dispatched by a gentle colourful trinity
Locket astounds with love for its likeness
(The priests are waiting across the night-time)
Egypt and Icarus launch a questing
The reed of enchantment promises sanctuary
Chimes are for children learning legato

A wretch of blackness polishes longings
But only a prince will redeem the bounty
By fond liberation of darkness's daughter
Wisdom is music for creatures to listen
And lust is jinxed by dance from its duty
Confession opens the cloth of justice
The duel for custody clears a hurdle

They face one another but trial by terror
Must first secure their holier happiness
Muteness must battle with every temptation
(Speech is the scourge of inner enlightening)
The savage triumph of silence batters
The waiting passion but will is witness
A chord suspends for a sun still sleeping

Mother avenger commands the moment
The priest-pretender must perish by dagger
But child once more concedes her commission
Virtue can tolerate nothing of vengeance
Instead the test is to climax acutely
The girl would now put paid to her living
So would the birdman but three prevent them

Flame and the torrent are challenged and chosen
And music protecting vanquished utterly
The passage taken the temple admits them
(Peace and its Wisdom are waiting patiently)
The couple are cleansed to combine forever
Villainy's minion are conquered and vanish
A choir of angels joyfully unison

VIII *Chorus*

To Constanze, Baden

I am just now returned from the opera,
It was fully attended as ever before;
The *duetto* 'Mann und Weib' etcetera
And the glockenspiel item in the first Act
As well as the Act II boys' terzett
Received the usual encore;
But it's really the evident *quiet* approbation
Which pleases me most of all:
Clearly in the public's estimation
The opera's rising rapidly, steadily, more and more.

IX *Canon*

There is a stranger standing at my door,
A gaunt, tall man clad in a cloak of grey.
He says that I must help him, and I know
There is no question of it. Yesterday

A gaunt, tall man clad in a cloak of grey
Appearing this way would have made me wince,
There is no question of it – yesterday
I was a different man, I am convinced:

Appearing this way would have made me wince
Into my looking-glass, for I believe
I was a different man. I am convinced
A death is imminent … I will not bleed

Into my looking-glass for I believe
The time has come to sign my settlement:
A death is imminent. I will not bleed
Or languish now – I will compose again.

The time has come to sign my settlement
(The mirror clouds) and I must seize the loss
Or languish now. I will compose: again
I will address my Maker with my notes.

The mirror clouds and I must seize the loss,
To consummate a lifetime faithfully.
I will address my Maker with my notes.
There is a Requiem awaiting me.

To consummate a lifetime, faithfully,
The cryptic messenger has set my task:
There is a Requiem awaiting me,
I must obey, nothing is left to ask,

The cryptic messenger has set my task.
He says that I must help him and I know
I must obey; nothing is left to ask.
There is a stranger standing at my door.

X *Strings*

Another dawn is slowly inflating,
I sense the shudder (the world is waiting)
Of sky and steeple, of mud and madness,
Continents stretching – I am Atlantis,
I am a worm in the dust of an ember,
I am a king, my life is wine,
I am a snowflake lifting December,
I am a pauper, I am divine.

But what if the mouth and mind of a creature
Can *not* be read by a God above –
Illiterate God no prayer or preacher
Can move: just music and love …
And is the sleep of God ever crammed
With nightmare dreams of the souls of the damned –
A chasm of voices waiting immensely?
(*If they should ever rise up against me …*)

Before we know it a lifetime scatters,
The highest wisdom straddles a bluff:
Everything matters and nothing matters.
Not to look back is not enough.

XI *Codetta*

To Constanze, Baden

... *Adieu* my dear,
my only love!
Hold your hands out in the air –
2999½
little kisses are flying from me
to you, and waiting to be
snapped up ...

XII *Lacrimosa*

He lies on a bed across from an instrument,
a pale plain face, betrays the glint
of fever, the chaos of concentration.
A candle, solitary, waves and wanders,
the eyes are shining – otherwise darkness.
He seems to be trying to sing, but suddenly
falters, shuffles, a sheet of paper
drops to the floor. He seems to be weeping
softly, bitterly. Someone is praying.

And it must be late for the night is silent
behind a window sealed and curtained;
a man and a woman are hovering closely,
she sits, he paces, she wipes his forehead.
Between the moments a clock is ticking
precisely, darkly, its arms are straining
to touch the zenith; a distant carriage;
someone has entered or someone is leaving,
or is it some shadow crossing discreetly …?

And look! The face, with its skin and stubble,
a taste of something dark on its tongue,
the nostrils flared, the fingers swollen,
the body burning and drugged with pain …
And could he be muttering, whispering something?
Slowly the wall is turning towards him,
a breeze from somewhere brushes the table
gently, a page of the almanac flickers
and turns to betray the morning: the fifth of

December 1791.

The Waterline Poems

Però, se 'l mondo presente disvia,
  in voi è la cagione, in voi si cheggia ...

Manifest

Science advances, evolution crawls,
the calendar propels the moon before it;
we celebrate direction, forwardness, the line
of letters or the dancing torrent
tabloid and broadsheet bring as evidence
against those vacuums we abhor, sameness
and silentness, the enemies of time;
and time becomes the prisoner of clocks.

Here we accost the all-consuming sea
of platitudes: that Character advances,
that Age gathers its wisdom naturally,
a kind of garland for the years of chances –
missed, when you track it out. And in the end,
tapered to pain, or glory, or to madness.

Descent: Below the Waterline

They say the drowning man about to die
experiences the flooded mind unreeling
frame by escaping frame the history
of every act and circumstance and feeling,
until the culmination of a lifetime's blindness
brings a release of momentary sight
and a perspective unalloyed and timeless
at that last instant of receding light.

I wouldn't know what it is like to die –
all too precise, time will devise its reckoning;
but I detect, when molecules of day
carry me to the ocean-face of dreaming
and night implodes its inky lullaby,
the past's peculiar vistas, beckoning ...

Schooldream

I ran the gauntlet of the years that night,
from first-day kindergartens of an alien food
and brown-smirched toddlers with befuddled legs
through bus-time bullies on the Old South Head
returning from a gruelling primary day
of Englishless encounters by a globe
turned always with the bulging reds in view
for apathetic strangers who could speak.

Then on to nervous corridors of chance
and lizard-tongue retractions from the cane
and useless Wednesday football masquerades
and lessons fraught with mathematic calm ...
Always before me, like a pair of specs,
the looking-glass horizon steaming up.

Heroes from the Line

Images dancing: my *Rienzi* Batman
flashlit across the Wintergarden skies,
George Reeves's crinkled 'S' (I nearly cry
to learn his bitter fall), at 8 p.m.
I'm sprinting home, my supercilious cape
streaming behind this overcrowded head,
the swell of flight rotating like a tape
that I alone can hear ... Or reconstruct instead

another turn of time: the coin is tossed
and lands on the reverse, I'm on the homebound
bus from school (it's 1958),
the swimmer Barry, big boy from next door,
is there to protect me as I disembark,
the daily bully sulks. Tomorrow, Barry will drown.

Back

My schools were rich in fashions, passing fads.
Sausage balloons – a thousand at a time
in every colour and all possible shapes
would decorate the playground in the sun:
a twist, a squeak, and *anything* emerged!
Then there were Tarax bottletops, flicked with the thumb
and middle finger like a blowfly sling.
Or plastic waterpistols – all that sort of thing.

What about yoyos, dizzying the grounds –
every kid's wrist and knuckles spelt prestige
or poverty; and the marble pits
flogged from the dirt or concrete with a throat
like barkers at the Show; and swapcards too,
Atlantic, Shell – but that's really going back ...

Blades

The circle was described within the sand,
the sand was moist and thick and solid-packed,
the packed-up penknife glistened in his hand,
the hand unscissored it in one glib act.
The act was slick and steady, and precise –
precisely as a razor he dispatched
the patch of earth the penknife cut, a nice
and nicely chosen slit, a challenge matched.

Above it all I recollect the *thwup!*
and *thwup!* of steel, its hiss into the soil,
a soil that could be aimed at from the up
upon a range of angles, with the coil
of coiling finger on the blade or wood.
I'd redescribe that circle if I could.

Waterline Sunday

Sun-filtered voices, a dazzle of sand,
my mother watching with suspicion from the edge,
I snorkel face-down in the north-end rockpool
examining crab-holes in the slippery ledge:
bodies about me, a murk at the bottom,
my face-mask is pressing, my nose laps the water
that rocks in the rubber, my lips like a clamp.
Sun-filtered voices, a sliver of land ...

For one split second I must have submerged
or been vanished, enough to arouse her panic:
I spotted her awkwardly splonk in the shallows,
more helpless than anything *I* might have struck
in my Sea Hunt, for she couldn't swim ...
(That's when I surfaced, and waved from the brim.)

Jailbait

Mucking about on the pier one afternoon
my friend and I, jointly inspired or singly,
decide to disconnect an unsuspecting dinghy
and start to paddle, our target the moon-
fat splendid flying-boat bobbing at its Base.
Welcomed aboard, we politely case
all the amenities, beaming at our luck,
then turn to take the borrowed vessel back.

That's when the royal rug is cleanly wrenched
from under us – when we reach the hatch
a detective is waiting. In some consternation
we're whisked by police car to the scowling station
then on to incredulous parents ... But before all that
I'm made to row the stolen vehicle back.

Light on the Waterline

Observe the little coracles of doubt
bobbing and bubbling on the tranquil waters.
Their mother is life; in a lurid cloud
death is the father cossetting his daughters.
He is destroyer, disbeliever, thief
of protections gathered in the moment;
she is creator, artist of belief
in honesty of mirrors and the cleansing torrent.

Suffer to question, struggle after peace;
doubt, to inherit clarity of knowing;
but clamber to be certain, and you cease
to suffer growth, merely continue rowing
in circles of an ever-swirling fiction:
the circular Sargassos of conviction.

Chess

On Tuesday nights you sat the School of Arts
in Bondi Road – blackjumper nights of chess
across a trestle-table scene of devious thoughts,
coffee, Scotch Finger, cigars in your face; as well,
some other thing discovering itself,
a reaching out of doors, even the way your shoes
resounded at the top of the old stairs,
and the romance of boards and clocks, new clues

swelling your steps – for all the time, of course,
things not of chess co-equal on your tongue:
intoxication of the railway crowds, the crazy clinging
jeaned impossibilities, the night
faces you turned into a pillow, or that other mood
welling superbly as you whispered *J'adoube!*

Fistgame

I am the earth, given identity
in three dimensions of compressed desires;
great dullness and a weight distinguish me
from his acuter wit; but since my mass
must overpower his thrust even as he
outshines, outraces me in daytime's dazzle,
I shall blunt him yet; and as for her,
she whom his nature constantly must scar,

I'm powerless to brave her folding sweep,
her delicate embrace and perfect skin
that creases as if pained to gather me
and close about my roughness like a womb.
And if she lives in terror of his reach,
she recreates and multiplies; I merely teach.

Juvenilia Waters

And every night I'd settle into bed
or sit myself under the table lamp
to carve another poem in my black
book with the faint blue lines traversing it,
each neat consecutive undrafted find
entered spontaneously, numbered, dated, signed:
a splendid casual arrogance of will
coupled with some evidence of unfolding skill –

those improvised enjambments where an impulse rowed
and rhymed and divided, ultimately caught
up with its logic or resolved its part
while all along a theme or thread cajoled,
cavorted, sank, or blandly transformed
itself; made drunken by that first flush of art.

Timescape

Figleaves are falling in the thicket now
the torch-bound carpenter climbs a stool
a gash of lightning precipitates a vow
condemning a millennium, and the Fool
fiddles with insects that the birds dispense
to prove a lie or vindicate a nesting
but poison arrows do a drawing-board dance
while Saint Sebastian watches unprotesting.

Chapters of marriages are silent as churches
a harmony of incense purifies the air
worship is perfume to the dreamers' urges
ten million blanknesses observe a square.
All across continents animals are queuing;
excuses are dying, whatever else they're doing.

Scrypt

There was a poet who had written one
fine work of art but nothing else beyond.
Try as he might, no further poems came,
no inspiration opened up the fond
sky of the soul to filter through his pen.
Think of the paper and the ink he'd spend
as he contrived in heightening despair
to recreate that momentary flair.

Nothing arrived – the muse was mystery.
What could he do? He struggled to forgive,
tortured his conscience, cleansed its history;
and every night, pretending to relive
that first, jardinian glimpse of the divine,
rewrote his only poem, over and over again …

Waterline

The comedy advances, we withstand,
to find ourselves prone on a golden beach
fastened with ligaments, our feet in sand-
castles constructed prehistorically, and each
digit a memory to be wiggled at,
each clump a lifetime sliding out of reach ...
And as the world proceeds with crooked gait,
we thrash about for causes, or we wait.

Here we rejoin the all-absolving sea
of alibis the calendar advances:
that Time unravels forward, or that History
was nothing but a plague of backward glances.
And as the pathway narrows up ahead,
we glance over our shoulder, and we tread.

Beyond Nietzsche

*... an infant's littlest, purest love: the kind
born of the moment, not the mind.*

I

Tonic/dominant, tonic/dominant ...
One ambulance crushes a thousand ants,
dozing pedestrians pass, or gaping
blunder against each other. A distinguished
father prides himself on self-control, is
irritated, drags his daughter
into a doorway. Tantrum unleashed
he desperately tugs, she lashes out, strikes:
he stuns her with a blow that breaks
his heart for weeks.

Across the road a poet, drunk
in the act of a risky procreation,
pauses. A siren is headed
for a fire, he lifts a shutter
like a half-meant apology, recalls a poem
he never wrote, returns
to his mug of scotch, the corpse
hot to his hand, his aetiology. *The Age
of Reason* hovers half-open by the bed,
her breath is thick.

A list of ants attack
a jamstain on the sink. I drum
the hollow stainless steel to startle them,
they scatter. Finger lightly licked
I pluck the stragglers, flick them in the grass
out the back door. Later
(three a.m.) my baby son squirms
like an insect at my neck.
How easily your children can expose you,
if you listen.

II

Like the stick sun of a small child
every word announces a spindle
of meanings.

An oboe's rim is riddled with minutest creatures;
the calligrapher's sac dispenses
a death-black fluid. Home with child
the heart of Übermensch is bursting
with goodwill: he listens to Requiem K.626
on his gramophone, ponders the meaning
of its dark beauty.
                    Tonic/dominant ...

Like the rippling pebble of a gazing child
each note unlocks a sun system
of meanings ...

III

But the ripples will quickly subside,
only the stone will know the weight of the water.
A spiderweb is infinitely trivial:
sitting and patiently waiting,
only the spider ...

So every meaning conspires against itself
till the littlest love alone can defy meaning,
and every word that makes the world
is half a moon hiding among absent stars.
      Each truth is a half-moon;
            the minutest love alone can escape meaning.

IV

And the galaxies – how swiftly they flick past
on the black train
torpedoing unalterably across the night
in the next suburb ... It is possible
the shriek that disintegrates a dream means
merely whistle, and a train,
isn't it?

I know a world
where every truth shelters a thousand lies,
each noble thought holds off a swarm of savages
again, and every smile disturbs
a labyrinth of doubts ... Familiar world.
Sometimes, alone at night
listening for trains, I hear its ghostly dialectic.
       Tonic/dominant, tonic/dominant ...

And I long for a word free of all its meanings.
       The littlest love.

from *Infinite City*

(1999)

House

Picture the scene: a house, two floors,
Two rooms, two couples couple quietly,
The upstairs bedroom darkened entirely
Except for a candle above the door
Next to the calendar curled in a frown:
The nineteenth century closing down.

The downstairs room: images jump
On a plastic screen in the gathering dawn.
She sighs – for a moment the man looks up:
His mother's mother is about to be born.

Memento Mori

The future came early that year
and the rains lacerated. After we said
goodbye on the surreal platform,
our faces melting as the steam rose off the rails
like some hissing spirit and the world
lumbered away from my vanishing point forever,

your remarkable eyes still hovered
where a steel wall had stood a moment back
but was now all white sky and smoke. I watched
the diminishing stack, hated its thin hysterical music.

Don Giovanni's Prayer

Grant me the way up the inclined plane
Of the imagination, show me how
All those dusty pyramids were constructed,
How you prevent the great stone sky from sliding,
Explain how marble can be bound
To mud, the mocking arrogance of towers; explain

The underocean's dark resolve, recalculate
A fishbone's vintage (be exact), render
The dazzle of knowledge in a woman's bed a constant
Possession. Teach me self-love. Surrender.

Time

You move among the rows and passages
without a thread – the maze cannot be bent
back on itself, only improved upon.
You weave and speculate – no inkling of its shape
or the direction of the corridors
conducting you, incontrovertibly,

from one side to the next. Sometimes you gaze
up, but you cannot see. Yet from this height
your labyrinth lies open like a tomb. My fingers itch
to trace your footsteps to the waiting gate.

Chess

A candle is dribbling beside the board,
the wax resembles a melting Rook,
a Bishop is crossing to find my palace,
a Pawn steps forward, the Knight that took
the Queen to task manoeuvres; the word
goes out – I hoist my chalice

and 'Check!'   Something enforces focus,
the eyes draw level the eyes unite
as if in a mirror, something awoke us:
my King is white, your King is white.

The Castle

The ruined castle contains a spiral staircase
winding into a turret lost in cloud.
The climber, 40, presses upward, coil by coil,
but he can glimpse no destination for his toil,
circling instead as if entwined about
some illusion of Escher's. Finally the place

is crossed where the climber disappears
into the mist; the stones settle in their tunnelled hive.
The tower will wait another forty years
for the infant born this moment to arrive.

Linkage

A spider of keys squats like a crossroads, plotting
your next move. The sundayness of an afternoon
going down in dust, ochre, the squalls of children
beyond streets that smoke quietly in their knowledge.
Stale infatuations nuzzle memory, oh such decades
late. A hint from the chill regions behind Scarlatti.

There are moments when lines intersect, when time
gathers itself into a bundle of arrows in the fist
of some god of ironies or nostalgia; when the book
drops with a remembering thud.

The Infinite City

The Infinite City extends in every direction.
There are boulevards, avenues, galleries, lanes, canals,
Gateways, courtyards, corridors, stairs and steps,
Intricate half-lit chambers. There are no exits.
The passages lead inward into density and madness
And out towards complexity and shape. Or the reverse.

From above, it is a neverending labyrinth,
From beneath, a spectacular sky: a fluid allegiance
Of light, shadow, sound, movement. From within,
An endless library of maps unfolding time

Cabaret

It's late and stuffy, the cigar-smoke is acidic,
the air is thick with sweat and sex and history,
you're in the audience, alone at a circular table
puddled with beer, sticky with apprehension,
you've come in here to watch yourself performing
up on that little stage, next to the piano.

You've folded yourself into this dim little corner
hoping you hadn't noticed yourself arriving
to spoil the surprise. You swivel nervously.
The lout who let you in is winking again.

The Desk-chair

One day the thought police arrive at your door.
You let them in, offer them scones and coffee,
making a neat display of being clean;
but they start snooping around –
in shaded corridors, rooms you'd forgotten to dust
and jammed cabinets stuffed with old letters.

You smile dismissively, reach for the icy slivovitz,
pour, shift in your desk-chair, produce a list
of platitudes. It doesn't help. Peering over a shoulder
you spy the mechanical parrot, laughing at you.

The Jester

Poet, astrologer, joke-teller, fool, bandit,
I'm the forgotten piece. Back in the days
When a board had eighty-one squares, I used to stand
Between my King and my Queen. The ways
I could move were various, and always curved;
I suppose the symmetry of battle was disturbed.

Oh, I still heckle one-liners from the gods
But you'd never know it. Everything's black and cream
To these wooden committees. While they push and prod,
A field of one hundred squares is what I dream.

Art

Having put the final touches to his landscape,
And remembering Van Dyke and Mary Poppins,
The tortured painter latched the windows, ate
The onion dip and drank his two last coffees,
Typed up a sorry note, retyped, tuned his guitar,
Checked the level of lotion in his jar,
Jotted down a poem (on what depression is),
Took a running leap – and rebounded with a jolt!

He'd forgotten he was an abstract expressionist
Whose landscapes lacked a vanishing point.

Faking It

Art should inspire an erection in the soul,
Cocteau said somewhere. That declaration
Has a nice ring to it, but it raises a whole
Bedlam of questions as to, well, consummation.
What, for example, should we dare to expect
Hard on the heels of the newly erect –

Spasm, conception, just a fleeting sensation?
Can we practise safe art? If not, how do we treat it?
And let's not forget: sometimes, bad improvisation
Can be justified simply by being repeated …

Extended Cadences

While on the artists' subject: I've been told
he's an utter genius at the immortality game –
knows just exactly what's in a name,
precisely when to recover from a nine-garret cold
for an opening. Yet his imagination seems poor:
he'll work for hours unirritated by a coathanger
    clecking on his door.

And he can sit with his sweetheart from sunset to eleven
diphthonged against a golden notwithstanding sky
flicking raindust off their lapels, making each other cry,
invoking the Lord; and he all the time wondering,
    which art in heaven …

Mona Lisa

No Nat, it's not a smile to tempt a lover,
I'm past all that. In fact it's many moods, they alter
imperceptibly: sweet longing for a land I'll never see
again, the glaze of boredom, and a gentle mockery
(my one defence left) of the puzzled eyes of all these
voyeurs who've trooped to Paris one thing on their minds,

to stand and outstare me for all the wrong reasons.
You're probably right about the broken heart.
I'm sick of this city, weary of its seasons:
cold, lonely and lovely? – *Dimmi*, what price art?

Oasis

There is an imaginary café not far from here.
Sometimes, when the sky is full of diminished chords
And the clouds illuminate a remarkable sunset,
I am not entirely unlikely to frequent it,
Studying one brown coffee after another, waiting
For a particular word to pronounce itself.

On days when I refuse to show up,
The round little waiter in the corner must imagine
Me and my open briefcase. Almost, almost,
He can hear my spoon dancing, so cleverly.

Galatea

It's worst when he lugs me to his bed at night:
The soft clammy flesh, the sweaty fumbling,
Those flabby encroachments. Yet the eyes haunt me.
'Oh, hold me, hold me!' he whimpers, pathetically,
Though he knows my paralysis – all I can do
Is gape unblinking at the stony ceiling.

Afterwards he'll always caress me lovingly,
Polish my thigh with a garland of tissues,
Then dwindle to a snore. I slip the blankets
And stand in the rain. Stand there imagining skin.

The Date

Each war contains all earlier wars,
Canetti says. The Father considers this,
the Daughter minces past the compact disc
repository snaked out across the shelf next to the door,
tossing a cruel eye. Her lipstick clatters proudly
from her lips into her side-slung armoury,

the bustle slams into a sudden truce,
he stops the book. Jammed on last night's news
the video timer flashes, the frame waits paralysed:
a girl with blood on her lips, war in her eyes.

Histories

Two glinting armies flex out across
    A desert's dotted line. The globe observes.
Two men that count compute the loss
    In capital and blood. A wrestler serves
Two women in a restaurant. Their heads are aligned,
    Their shadows trap what solace they can find.

    A couple cling to one another's dream,
Two children climb a staircase like a bruise.
    Another history opens. Through the steam
Two faces stare into a troubled mirror. Whose?

The Journey

And the star turns cold on him and goes
Out, and the throat constricts on bedwinter dawns
And all those interviews on drive-time radio confirm
Incomprehensibility of what used to be
So natural: ambition, the blind drum, scaling the ranged hills
Without blinking – momentum of the complexities, really.

And the chin wears a path over the shoulder,
The belly settles on brown granules, white powder, children
Console, drive-home-time consoles – the journey not,
This cobbled expressway of signs and blackening holes.

Vespers

Two men are cogged in a tall conversation
by the side of a solo lingering car. Their shadows
and the shadow of the finned limo
steaming in a dusk of delayed departures
claw forward diagonally across the parking lot's
cooling Gotham, hoping nobody notices.

Nobody notices the day slowly moving off.
The two, the machine between them, laugh, a laugh
lost on the yellowing day and already sad as history.
A metallic cadenza warns of a nearby tower.

The Hair

Strolling fondling the *Guide* and glad he bought it
he flattens ants below his knowledge / the mouth soon sings
as he cooks / he swallows a warm slice of slaughtered
mammal and a bum of bird for dinner / brings
an axe killing and the latest balaclava rapes to screen
with coffee / takes the news depicting the impressive scene

of a military massacre plus the latest promise
fifty thousand in the Persian quakes / yawns / to quell it
he retires to dream of nipples / next morning nearly vomits
when a razor hair gets caught on his palate.

Safe Purchase

A rusty smile, a nature
limited by physiognomy,
he slides inside the store,
slouches near the suntan desk,
tries on some purple specs
and one Akubra-type device,

chuckles like a gate, comes
to the quiet counter, coughs,
pays with a big note for a small
pack of orgasms. Cleanly goes.

Liberian Seaman

Punched the revolving gate into the great department
store at the crazy skyline's heart, and smiled,
a little akimbo, the lips in a gash like Gambia,
taking in the gross map of his planet, the kids
oozing with heat, the kaleidoscope of smells
merging into a single hungry glaze. Twisted

the elbow to nudge the blaster down to the boards,
snapped off the music-muffs, jabbed at a fat rusty pair
of sausages rhyming under hot glass, flipped a two-buck disc
and attacked, the lips clamped in a Senegal of a smile.

The Note

Savaged at the skirts by a terrier toddler
yelping a tongue of rage she alone
translates, she alone, she the one mad lunge
away from public loss, she the one
arbitrary breath from private break,
savaged, cracked, is astonished to detect

a drawn-out half-inhuman howl
filling out like dye the supermarket aisle,
a wail into whose pedalpoint she very slowly
tunes, to claim it as her own.

Winding Up

He scowled. Putting down the plastic receiver
to the way such men get in the hi-finance pie
he flicked his very least assuming tie
out of its rack like a recuperating diva
before that furious fax to the Bankruptcy Board
went off and he to the corner Shop

to keep a date: the pricy one in the purple pants
who kissed, his favourite. Climbing the 'case,
'One helluvaday,' he purred, 'but Progress,
let's see if *I* can corner some of *you* for once!'

Narcissus

In the end, of course, he got married
to himself. A civil ceremony, nothing too glib, a friend
or two, a reporter from the *Mirror*, the odd flame
from the past, a waiter with icy water;
his watery parents, a little perplexed, looking around,
confused because no engagement had been announced.

The celebrant was vague, her words left an eerie
echo, she quickly left. Nobody spoke. At last, he escorted
himself into the Bridal Suite: nervous, a little beery,
he sat there blushing on the edge of a single bed.

Office Party

Well now, what Christmas prezzie would please her?
He rummages in the cupboard, turns
His surviving stockpile upside down, burns
His lip on a luke cigarette – a sneeze
Arrives. He sneezes. Pollen! ... Growing glum:
Eternally scraping the barrel's bum ...

She hasn't got a sexy thing to wear. The boss
At first will just want her to listen, but she'll toss
Off all the predictable barbs. Later, to make amends,
She'll crumble in his Christmas pudding hands.

Water Music

Trapped in a rainy car, I am conducting
The Berlin Philharmonic Orchestra with concise
    Passion. The Scherzo has just reached
        The intersection of Wattletree and South,
I soar into the vinyl ceilingwork and bump
My head and bite my tongue a bit;

My wrist flows back like a tide – I feel
    The English horns are always so mellow here.
        Rounding the curve into the Rondo finale I feel
My feet on the pedal podium starting to itch.

Homo Singularis

He would drive his car on the wrong side
of the seat, tried to obtain a licence to kill
time, at work he displayed considerable skill
at incompetence, at home he had to hide
the dismissal notes under the mattress he screwed
to the carpeted floor with nails. Rude

he was to a fault, nosey to boot,
inconsiderate to snails, he locked himself into books
of stamps and common prayer, funnelled his looks
into singles bars and hardly ever stepped foot
inside a song. Even his poems were too long.

Outrageous Fortune

Beatrice kept a couple: one in her bonnet
And one in a jar with a pierced yellow lid. On it
She'd inscribed in her blackest superlative italic
Her fat pet's moniker, Bee-Bee. Now, Beatrice's metallic
Diction was passable, but her stutter was appalling.
One day an aunt she had insulted, instead of calling,

Slotted a note, scrawled with an old stub –
While the insect stumbled about in its buzzing tub.
Oh, the sting of that message when Beatrice turned the key:
'And how might your tubby bee Bee-Bee be, Bea?'

Bless Relaxes

Those avuncular fathers of the Fifties
    knew nothing of J. Alfred's visit.
That they never looked particularly descript is
    the failure of art – or is it?
And the girls in their frilly fifty-eightness
    were clean as cream, and whiteness,

And things that went click when they closed,
    like kisses and criminals' faces,
And the pants always falling off of those ...
    As Blake once said, 'Damn braces'!

Lullabies

Our two heroes lie, cheat, brawl, maim, rapine
a path through another pathetic sleepy western verismo,
joined by this background banjo that's homely and merrily
takes up the spirit so it must be OK –
can't we see these are colourful high-flying naturals
jus' lettin' off steam? – the music says so.

Or, here comes ole Indy, and a hundred corpses
go flying behind him in every direction,
and there rides the anaesthetist, his music stirring
our daydreams; smilin', we sleep.

Flash Pan

IBM and Coke to sponsor *Did God Act Alone?* –
a six-day Docudrama with some startling revelations.
The Muscovy pope to file a Dispensation
confirming her rank as the seventeenth Chessperson.
Babel redeclared a multicultural Fiasco.
Marx spotted by Dante above a Monopoly board

while Nero Claudius Caesar etcetera burns.
Bishop takes Queen Cleo, they impose
Esperanto on the leaning Tower. Time turns, Rome goes
out. The Sphinx, too riddled, can't really tell.

Historian

His moral prose is semicolonized; it seems
    to rise and fall like some ethnic dance.
Whenever I ask him what the hell it all means,
    he fumbles: 'Um,' and 'Ah,' he says.
So I ask about the lowest point in history,
    and why he won't ever reread his books.

'Third Reich, no more magnetic mystery require!'
    Then he gives me one of his semicolon looks,
    it's late. 'When evening does a Roman Empire
I tremble in the dark.' And, 'Makes the print fade.'

Syzygy

What I connote is both conjunction
And opposition, I'm where the moon
Meets the sun; I'm a combination
Of two feet in a measure, an immov-
Able union, or a cluster of functions;
A couple of linked things, or their relation …

Yet sometimes the other s's gang up on me,
They mock my vocalic rut, my rash of descenders,
They call me *Three-y's*, and remind me I'll always be
The last … Who cares! Yesterday, I met Xystus.

Meeting of Minds

Just because her fingers tap at the wheel
Precisely in tempo to mine, while we stand stopped
To stare at the lights, what possibility she'll
Be tapped into a tape : jazz : trumpet : Davis : *Kind
Of Blue* : first song first side
                      ('So What') ?

And then even supposing such a megamillion-to-nothing
Shot came home, what can the actual chances
That her tapping to the mentioned composition dances
At the very location mine does be ?

Imperfect Rhymes

'A little uneven' – this most elastic dictum
is paradigm for the elasticity of tongues. A little
like the umpire raising his finger to dismiss
a fly, a little like attempting to explain
pitched outside leg stump or the Eureka Stockade
in Polish, a bit like a surgical strike.

Language, like ink, deceives. Poor little February
is fielded by two thirty-ones – go on, indulge your
connections. A little obscure? My point, thank you very
much! Today even ink is plastic. Uneven ink: nostalgia.

Smoke '62

Am studying a panoramic shot of an eastern suburb,
discern the street, the corner house, our first Holden,
the nearby park with a delicious stab through the heart;
am a time-travelling spy satellite homing right in now,
reframing, enlarging: the house zooms into focus,
am peeling away roof, reopening lost boxes …

A man with a frozen armchair gesture observes
his stalagmite of smoke, a woman turns from the kitchen
her hands in steam, a boy in the front study smoking a pen
stares straight into the future.

They Sing

There are some histories my mother won't discuss,
certain things on TV that upset her;
but she offers me three poems, she composed them
a life ago, Blechhammer, Peterswaldau;
I tenderly retype them (recall the cool green Remington,
my lists of Capitals, the 36 Presidents, the Top 40).

They sing. My father can sing too, can recite
reams of Polish poetry by heart. Sometimes
she pretends she's asleep when I come home late,
'Pictures of Matchstick Men' on my car radio.

The New World

My father is walking his ladder,
He is repainting the steep rectangular room
Walking his ladder along the wall like stilts
To save dismounting each time he needs to move it.

The rocking drum of paint is notched with valleys
Like a seismograph, the earth flashes past
Under my father's overall straddle,
He is thinking about something; an undercoat
Abandons his brush like blood,
Shaming the old room with its brash whiteness.

The Keys

My little son is selecting his letters
with the care of a novice connoisseur;
he hesitates, holds down 'Shift', drops
a steep finger to the chosen key, then
checks to admire the progress of his line.

My daughter's fingers skip and speculate,
the line she forges floats above the lull
of the piano-room; arpeggios by old Bach,
chords by the boy Mozart. And I crouch
behind WordPerfect's mirror, making this.

Chalkmarks

The desk calendar reveals the purest zen,
or else a tragedy old as Eden. For instance,
first you compile the angular days, and then
you watch them shorten; feign a resistance
right down to the absurd, knowing the day
will come when the day won't come, the way

the face darkens, the way it's no longer
possible to live life to the letter.
What can remain though is something stronger,
a lighter knowing: like chalklight, operetta.

Against the Grain

So you reckon the mirror looks away,
    the corridor turns into an endless circle,
    the maze comes out at its beginning,
    time double-crosses the shell you mistake
    for an echo curling at your ear.
But listen! Where did that rustle come from?

    I'll put it like this: the travelling hourglass,
    its twinned parabolas, the essence flowing –
    these are reflections that won't betray you.
But stand on your head, and the sand falls upwards.

Glissando

From a train, each act is slowed, made trivial
    in a sadness outside duration. That's the real
wisdom of trains … You hurtle past a suburb: men limp
    into doorways, schoolgirls stroll the sun, the street
vendors are statuettes with heavy mechanical limbs.
    Who was it said time is an engine of cogs and gears?

Look again. This crowded *shtetl* is no vanished world
    from the mists of time, sealed in monochrome sorrow,
but life, poised at the lit leading edge of time. A child
    waves, smiles up at us: as if there's no tomorrow.

Sunspots

The people have filled the city's open spaces,
they stand shoulder to shoulder, expecting everything.
The platform above the Square is empty.
A buzz of unease caresses the bare heads,
their coronas of hair thinning into the breeze;
see the rolled-up newspapers, the scarves that twitch.

The hum mounts to a whisper, the whisper
delivers its secret, the secret
is betrayed, spreads like an epidemic;
outside the city they are building a pyramid of books.

Millennium

The investigating magistrate, unprejudiced, has trod
The intersections of insanity and evil,
He has observed the alibis shouted across his century,
Has crawled through slashed minds of men like a weevil,
He understands thresholds, the dagger existentially
Throbbing in its glittering holster, the heat haze

Mounting towards midday, the urgent flies
Taking on a formality, like the whisper of God …
He remembers someone's chronicle, something it foretold:
Give me a prejudice and I will move the world.

Umbrage

I thought I had dispensed with you,
but I'd forgotten about noon.
A couple of moments past the zenith
you were back, at first no more
than a dark ripple around my feet,
a mute echo. One hour later

you were shadowing me again,
with characteristic *Schadenfreude*
mocking my translucent body,
sending up my see-through soul.

Night Journeys

Yes, he would plunder the stations into dawn
for vistas that shone between flickering pylons
before the tunnel overtook again; for reflections
other than his own in the tunnelled glass
black as recognition; for the tap on shoulder
that might soften, turn the lurid twilight

into a white pool of recognition, reunion. Yes,
he scoured the night, leaning out of his dreams,
reckless to swallow the hooting wind,
squinting to decipher the stations, the graffiti.

For Light

If one is to be awoken by a cliché
the clatter of breakfast dishes is as good
as any, or the aroma of coffee
freshly brewed, or that uncanny mood
of holiday immensity, when the world
was twelve, or a summer's garden when the world

was good. Worst is the midnight
phonecall, or the way the disentangled mind
can brood a black density into being –
in the darknesses before seeing, lusting for light.

Like Music

Between the grid-lines and the trenches of a plank of melody,
Above and below the ledger-lines of a labyrinth page
Of hollowed-out and blacked-in, propped and suspended planets,
Now separate now joined in perfect concatenations,
To the right and then to the left of the mysterious floriated
Twinings and entablatures – resides the sound.

It is the voice of heartbeat and of measuring and of death,
Song of the thousand infinite recombinations that push up
At the tangent, and at the point where lines slice one another,
The soul's ineffable singing. How it trembles, like music.

Omen

Then, all at once, all music stopped.
Loudspeakers the planet's length fell dead,
Discs and reels ran down in tacit unison
Redundant in their sockets, transistors blasted
Disembodied speech, orchestras squirmed
Foolishly, operas in mid-finale fell apart …

And then the birds ceased to arrive,
Great factories ground to a quiet standstill,
The languages began to run like watercolours;
The sea looked up, but the moon too was silent.

The Golem

I walk among you, breathing clay,
Everything I touch is smeared with red earth,
You who created me will not easily forget the day
Your computations and your magic gave me birth.
I shall fashion my earthen generations
After my own kind, we will conquer your vanity,

Transform you for your longed-for dispensation
Of harmony and bliss. But know this: the joy
Of paradise will demand your soul for the new sanity:
Whom we would make sane, we must first destroy.

Distorting Venice

What articles of what faith are left us –
Squinting for the ratios, mean-mouthed,
Mean-spirited, pinched of perspective,
    Imaginations gloved in the gum
    Of blueprints, relativities, the dog-star
Remote as pyramids, mean cynosure?

Where is the incandescence and the fever
Of careless knowledge, shining absolutely –
    Where Canaletto's astonishing frameworks
    Render their moralities, and suffice?

Untergang

There will be no flames
No final pestilence will inherit us
Great detonations will not tear asunder
The planetary crust, the oceans
Won't rise up to blanket us
In an oblivion opulent as time.

There will be no choruses of pain
No pyramids of bones, skeletons will not walk
As they once did – at the end of the world
Only the last child sobbing for its mother.

After Messiaen

At the end of time
There will truly be nothing left to say
We will all turn and walk sadly
Into ourselves, words will drift
Useless to the ground, defining for maybe
One last moment the old epochs of thought.

The final note of the last melody
Will coil up into itself, its overtones
Lingering deeply in the new silence
Folding into its edges like a dream.

Credo

And I really do believe in such a thing
As purity of heart, or degrees of it,
And in some Presence calibrating it,
And the scales being Music. I want to sing
The simultaneous truth of truth and illusion,
The city's endlessness, the soul's profusion.

A paper bookmark quietly considered
From the edge of a book seems lodged in its home
Of flimsy borderlines as if it
Belonged there, like a sword in stone.

from *The Man and the Map*
(2003)

from **Polish Corridors**

2

A roughneck yard,
a sandpit up the front
under the pantry window
on the second floor,
the monkey bar down
at the other end
I seldom seemed to share
with the other boys,
but in between
was the black smiling slot
of our communal tip,
sheltered
under its concrete
(or was it timber) overlying lip
ideal for clambering in,
keeping a lid
on the rude aroma
for those in the flats above
but magic to children:
we didn't mind
the rotting rubbish smell –
part of the fun,
all part of what you might
happen to find,
a serendipity
dependable as the sun.

3

My first brush with death
was the doorway roughly opposite
the tip – an acrid,
mysterious, unsettling
disinfectant smell
from an apartment somewhere
upstairs: forbidden
staircase. I recall as well
the warning emblem
on the wall: a skull
of death – in my first tongue
a name trembling
with untold dreadfulness;
I thought
of that special book
kept high above my reach
showing the photographs
of naked women
walking in long lines
for disinfection.
It made me strangely shy
the way they covered up
their private parts
with pathetic hands –
how foolish they must have felt.

4

On a Sunday I suppose
quietly I climbed
the stairs, stung
for some reason
I couldn't divine
by what I had been called.
The play-yard sank
into its cryptic dusk
behind my mounting something ache,
the playmates scattered
to their respective plates
of cabbage soup
and beetroot and potato broth
and steamed sinewy meat,
and tubs made hot by stoves
and coal, and candles
always standing by;
and so did I.
But as my mother, my father
flung wide the door
I balanced two questions
on my breath: one
might well have been
about that death,
but also
what was a jew?

Retracing the Map

'And that a circle may be described from any centre,
at any distance from that centre.'
— Euclid's *Elements* (Book I)

Scandinavia was always a beast springing,
    but quite unsavage — its soft Norway face,
the fluffy belly. Greenland kept growing,
    and Madagascar might nestle exactly
into the coastline of the Portuguese East.
    Ceylon was a tear displaced by India,
Great Britain sat there, aloof, triumphant,
    a hag with a prickly chick on its knee
neglecting Poland, buried and bloated —
    except along Danzig, its defiant splinter.
Italy reclined, obvious and easy,
    at the magical heart of the Mediterranean,
with Cyprus pointing into its corner
    to bypass Israel, that wedge in the middle
connecting the continents spun around it.
    The vectors of North and South America
were an artist's achievement — Canada slept,
    its head in cloudland, Alaska gestured,
Mexico spilt into mystical curlicues
    tied off at Panama, and the old four-dozen
a perfect jigsaw, with risqué Florida
    risking that finishing touch of genius.
Japan was a slippery-dip into China,
    a loop to nudge their Korean cousin,
Vietnam an innocent arrogant bristle,
    the Soviet Union resisted containment,
its shape impossible, and Africa's rhythm
    a miracle longing to nuzzle Brazil.
Across the bottom Australia was floating,

    never elusive, its bulk pretendless,
the ramshackle avian perched on its finger,
    the pointer at starboard craning to study it:
a weird balloon suspended from fragments,
    a bubble completing the world.

Observatorium

I dredge again into memory for the sweetness
    of the unattainable. It is a complex compass,
        it is simplicity itself. I rotate the dome
of the planetarium: scan the flashing firmament for home.

West is nostalgia, the pangs of history,
    the sweetest and most sacred, a miracle-land
        or lake of delight, regret, illusion: a territory
where time is eternally vanishing as it shows its hand.

East is perpetual motion, the old wheel
    and the new with its spokes lacquered, or studded
        with gems and pebbles, its rim covered
in cards: I prise them off each morning to reshuffle, redeal.

South is the night, the quaking of the ground
    and the blurring of vision, noisy report of a dim salute
        from the suburbs: welcome to the circumnavigating mute
armada patrolling the royal mosaic, the inverted crown.

North is the moment the needle urges, the unstillable
    longing for time that ceases to vanish, the all-answering hum
        when the wheel pauses, the tremors subside: a syllable
sounds the world, the diamond and the heart are one.

What time is it? Still daylight or the dark?
    My telescope is back where it began, full circle, stark
        in its outline against the shimmering vault.
Maybe the eyepiece is at the wrong end. That's not my fault.

The Wooden Box

Like a rhetorical question to which an answer is expected,
The wooden box inhabits the corner of my desk.

It's barely four inches by three, an inch and a half deep,
With a framed chessboard design roughly embossed on the lid –

Though the chess-grid is eight by *eleven*, a rectangular field,
Too many squares – you couldn't play real chess on this.

Besides, no fingers could properly clutch such miniature men
But a child's, or God's (and we know He's not interested in chess).

The box doesn't lock, the clasp won't even click. You *squeeze* it shut:
Chunky, tight as concealment – and the half-broken hinge

Doesn't help, a trick to open and close. Inside, in a cottonwool sac,
My mother's necklace of small coloured stones – too small

To be carved into miniature chess. Sifted and stirred in the half-open
Palm of my hand, they rustle, they whisper, like memory.

Passive Smoking

At seventeen or so,
in the days when just about everybody smoked,
especially over coffee and a game of chess,
I was a regular passive smoker.
The room was usually rectangular, or long,
with the trestles joined to form two parallel rows:
between these the competitors would pace,
awaiting a move, inspecting a neighbouring game,
passively feigning nonchalant total control –
they didn't need to sit it out, they needed
to show they were just coming in
for the kill. Probably it sometimes worked:
a quiet but showy focusing of choice,
a decisive nod, the attack (flowing but compact,
ultra-cool), a wrist flung with style
at the double clock, the move recorded, and then –
up in smoke, back into the alley of height …
Of course, it was different with Lightning,
and with Go – except for the smoke in your face.

Actually, I didn't mind – especially that
opening burst of sparks, ignition,
the aromatic whiff. It could
get tedious though, after a full-evening's worth.
I never played chess as a boy
but my father smoked, and abandoned it
many times – it took him half a century (or more)
to kick it away for good.
I used to watch him: once, perhaps I was six,
in the corner next to the second window
above the street, I set myself up
in his fauteuil, held open the daily print
(our *Tribune of the People*),
crossed my knees

– the stolen cigarette dangling from my lip –
and waited passively to be caught. It worked,
everyone laughed. That was the chair
where *Alice* and *Winnie* (with a Polish voice)
entered my world. I don't recall if he smoked
as he read to me – possibly so.
I don't believe he ever smoked in bed,
or not when I was there between them. Mum
never touched a cigarette, far as I know.

At university I'd sit on the steps
of the Menzies Library, waiting to bludge
or accept a fag from the first available friend,
watching the student girls in miniskirts and jeans,
watching philosophically the huge lawn
that rolled towards the Chancellery –
very passive. Probably nobody noticed how deep
and sophisticated I seemed,
how available for some ultimate romance. But
I hardly ever swallowed the smoke, not really
(although I tried, God knows),
plus I never actually *bought* a pack (my girlfriend
smoked a lot) – except just once, a soft bundle
of Stuyvesants, the fashionable brand.
But then, succumbing to an outbreak of good sense
that launched a legend, and having wasted
no more than one or two, I chucked
the symbolic pack in a cylindrical public bin
outside the law courts at Taylor Square
and haven't lit a tobacco cigarette since.
All right, there's the occasional iconoclastic cigar:
but that's a kind of chess! –
the smoke, the passive sweep, the portable glow.
All those gallons of coffee do the rest.

Legend

But this was 1969: her father seemed so old that
I expected him to crumple at any moment. Instead he folded

his fat Saturday paper, smiled Nixonically
and, thoughtful, brushed at his shadow like an alcoholic. 'We

eat at six on Saturdays, you're welcome to join us.
In the meantime, drive nicely.' At last: we were alone as

a couple of cosy parkers in Lovers' Lane, or almost – this was a
daytime date so we'd have to make do. And because her

Psych project was due Monday, and tonight being the night of
her babysitting debut, most of the weekend was a write-off.

So we drove down to this windy deserted beach
halfway along the coast, to a place where they'd converted each

little picnickers' bay into a sheltered virtually one-car
niche, turned off the wipers, the motor, managed to plunk our

starving bodies into the back, where, peeking over at
me like a magnet she loosened herself somewhat and 'Gopherit!'

she said. And before we knew it, as the cross-hatched rain
sealed us into our great dream forever, latched in our hot pain

against the wet world, half-naked where it mattered;
and as I watched her effigy unveil, and our teeth chattered

in the steam of the afternoon downpour, and she unravelled a
hand into my skin, and I sensed her perfect shadowy parabola

remould itself and disappear somewhere and grow ample,
and understood the thrall of Samson as he grasped the temple

pillars with all his love and all of his power; and as I knew all
this, I suddenly recalled, absurdly, that the fuel

gauge had been sitting on absolute zero and in a while I'd
have to restart the car; I thought of her dry old dad and I smiled,

and I looked into her spinning, half-open eyes and her arms clung
irreleasably and that was the moment I drowned, there among

the pounding waves of rain and her infinite lips … That and
the radio humming, and 1969; and who cares today if any of this

is anywhere near the way it never quite happened.

Quicksilver

'Unlike the angels, we forget our pleasures, and
repeat them.'
— Philip Salom

Each journey will begin with arrival,
Each destination will rekindle the blood
And its imaginings like a will to survival,
A membrane stretched between melody and mud.
The drunken song, superb, with its special effects
At the end, that you barely understand –
The way it rears its gorgeous head, like sex,
Each time you cup that radio to your hand –
Recurs eternally, yes, by invitation,
With magic pictures from the valley of dreams;
But when you try to pin down the notation
Quicksilver scatters from your touch, and gleams.
Like a triangle whose sides never meet,
The art of our necessities is strange indeed.

Ago

i
If not for the sweetness of the reward
If not for the delicacy of the superb fleeting instant
Would not our fumblings be absurd
Reaching for that instant of connexion

ii
It must have been a thousand years ago

iii
A glimpse
And something exquisite in that glimpse
A shape a turning a possibility a sweetness an idea
A reward in that glimpse
And the glimpse its own reward

iv
Here is a room
And here is a room
A thousand years ago
The room is six years old
With spots of dust drifting in the window light
And the room is twenty
With a secluded bed full of two strangers
Who know each other
A little

v
And here in between
Is a street of cats in the sweet impossible evening
A street eight years old
With two strangers
Under the swerving sky of stars

Too small to know what they cannot know
(But one of them knows he longs for something
He cannot know)

vi

And the room too was impossible
And its dust fluttered as it watched
Two strangers
Under the behaved ceiling of invisible dust
Too little to know what
(Though one of them knew he needed something to know
A sweetness a reward a glimpse
Only what)

vii

But the second room was not impossible
And the furniture
In the second room barely creaked
In the basement
In the dimmed basement of the forgetful house
And the two strangers
(Who knew there was a thing that longed to be known)
The two strangers who knew
Each other a little
Knew each other a little
Because there was so much that was impossible
In the instant that was fleeting
And superb

viii

A thousand years ago

ix

And the room was left behind
Buried beneath the dust of other rooms
And the street was abandoned to the cats

With the sky in their eyes
In the impossible evening

x
And the second room
Is dead
Shattered against the ancient cliffs
That longed too much to be known
(That waited for the thing that longed to know them)
And the sweetness
And all the moments of connexion
Are a glimpse a possibility
Its only reward

xi
And here is a room
A third room
In a house far distant from the house of drizzling dust
From the street of slinking stars
From the house of maps
That rustled as they spread over the furniture
But could never be refolded
Entirely
And would never be opened again.

xii
Not in a thousand years

Eclipse

for Gwen Harwood

Our memories stretch to fit us,
    extend our days
between one dream of darkness
    and the next.
Landscapes unsettle, we awake
    mysterious to seek
the compass of each myth until
    the shutters fall
and we climb back to the skin,
    elastic, and we ban
the riddles of the dark, murky
    terrain, the library
we can never quite locate, cave
    never quite leave.
We peer into the ever-fading map,
    the colours jump
into and out of focus; we devise
    colourful glories
and elaborate ghosts, or flecks
    of paradox
over the perfect irony of mind
    which is our bond
and hostage. Meanwhile, indistinct
    avenues connect
and disconnect, eerie vehicles ply
    their dim territory,
figures, voices foreshorten, bend
    beneath the wand
of contrapuntal sleep: we reach
    into dark, the latch
lifts or dissolves, the gate swings
    open, awkward songs

and longings visit us – we sleep,
    forget the drop
of knowledge trembling on one half
    of the fragile leaf,
the other perpetually dark, forever
    strange, forever
locked eclipse, just its silhouette
    serrated with light.

It

He walks the networks of my little city,
Swinging his lantern, crying out the time.
                                  – Evan Jones, 'Him'

    Flat on my back I listen to the dark,
Allow the effigies of day to settle
And disperse, call up the soothing current
    Down the extremities, await the start

    Of numbness: indiscernibly the torrent
Of sensations abandons the heart
And then the high ground of the fading battle,
    The field shimmers, familiar but foreign

    Designs coalesce, tantalize and scatter
As the undertow balances its clean burden,
Steadying for the golden hush when the Ark
    Will lift invisibly, hover above Ararat

    Again, its cable like a silver exclamation-mark
Still anchored in rock; and the beasts utter
A prayer, and the great sky is reopened,
    And the land is my shadow, as we drift apart.

Washington Pilgrim

(9 January 1999)

Not a snowfall in forty-two years and now DC,
Trudging the empty city dissolved in fog
Like a faulty memory, and the Senators convene
To topple a President. Down Constitution, across the park,
Past the Botanic Garden – the snows lie mounded,
Sidewalks slick as a spiral staircase lashed with soapy water,
The Hill a mereness of white sketched with slivers of twig,
The Capitol bubble a blank, deleted, indecipherable.
Up Independence toward the Library of Congress,
Its grand entrances cordoned off, the Supreme Court
Locked up, sleeping in. My camera collects it,
The fog weighs and will not lighten.

(Yesterday an amazing assembly of Lincolns
Gazed into the neat basement museum
At Ford's Theater – I browsed in reverence, quietly
Shot a nest of Honest Abes etched into canvas
And stone. You could virtually catch the first Johnson
Muttering from his once unassailable corner,
Proud still of his footnote, following the bizarre events.
A beggar directing traffic near 10th and E,
'It is very cold, sir.' So I'd handed him a quarter.)

The snow remembers itself, a wind awakens,
I shroud the Canon into my heavy coat, the camera bag
A weightless bandoleer, drag down the beanie,
Sidle into my gloves, tread against the clock toward 14th –
Where the Holocaust Museum trembles in sunless light,
Its inhabitants staring into the uncomprehending Now
Still waiting behind their stark installations,
Cold and resigned and long past nakedness.
An occasional cab fanning snow-spray into the gutter
On this day of history and good intention.

Mr Wilkinson

Patrolling the playground was a kind of God.
We adored his noble bearing, classical physique,
the absolute ease of authority. I was eleven.
His boots tapped out a superlative charisma
when he paced the asphalt – tall, calm, protective,
his coiled strength and razor glance enough
to paralyse any reckless challenge.

That year I befriended Klara – scrawny, sad,
refugee from a world we couldn't fathom.
What did my sunburnt aunts and elders know
about those funny foreign labels on her map:
Prague, Budapest, Bialystok, Dachau, Treblinka?
Klara knew. One April morning,
during a lesson in Geography – when Mr Wilkinson
would often unroll the rose-coloured countries,
how we belonged to the greatest living Empire,
our glorious victory in the recent World War –
Klara stood up. Her incipient English
could always send titters round the classroom,
but Mr Wilkinson was protective, calm.
On this occasion he'd been aiming his tall pointer
at the vicinity of Europe: each pupil
had to sing out the name of a famous capital,
whereupon Mr Wilkinson would instantaneously
click his neat cane to the precise coordinates
and recite the basic facts about the city,
its monuments, the land it stood for.

Klara stood up, the class tittered
and skewed its lazy interest in her direction.
She uttered, proudly, a strange three-syllable sound,
and 'My town!' in that halting music of hers.
The class waited. Mr Wilkinson paused,

then asked her to repeat it, and to 'speak up'
for the benefit of those who hadn't heard her.
She made the same odd word – *Varshava* – a little louder,
'The place, I'm coming from,' she added, looking lost.

Mr Wilkinson grinned. He let his stick subside
in an arc like a violinist, perpendicular
to the scratchy expectant desks.
The Queen stared down from next to the blackboard,
her mystic smile suddenly more exacting,
the flags of Australia and the United Kingdom
appraised one another from opposing front corners,
a breeze ruffled the notes about P & C meetings
pinned to the tacky corkboard near the door;
a blowfly circled the buzzing lamp that swayed
from the dead heart of the ceiling. Mr Wilkinson
sighed, hopped cleverly off the platform
and ambled down to Klara. 'We are doing
capitals only, Klara – you will have to *show* us
the exact location of your little town in Poland.'

Klara blushed, hesitated. He nodded towards the map
and perched on the edge of her desk as the girl strode
to the rolled-down Europe waiting up the front.
Then, in a voice sudden with indignation,
'Warszawa,' she announced. 'Is capital of my country,
biggest town in Poland, I'm coming from.'
She turned to the map and with the purest grace
swept her small hand deep into her homeland,
to caress the bold black label that said 'Warsaw'.

Just then the bell went, the usual rustle erupted,
we shuffled outside for Playtime and fresh milk;
but what I had glimpsed imprinted in that moment
on Mr Wilkinson's face has haunted me
for forty years. His smile was chalky, superior,
but the *eyes* – suddenly blank,

with an emptiness between mockery and loathing;
and what frightened me in that instant of exposure
was the eerie absence of light behind those eyes –
a colour that glinted, yes, but opaquely.
I recalled, absurd, those impossible horror stories
Klara told me, of men in black tunics
who grinned to machine-gun a column of ghost children,
then fondled tenderly a dog's silken ear …
Right on the bell another teacher had entered
and the shock of the crazy vision was dispelled;
but as the two of them shared a private jest
or passing pleasantry, Wilkinson's smile tightened,
his eye stood still, and I could almost sense
some terrible conspiracy, and understood
in that second elusive moment that Mr Wilkinson
was never again to be trusted,
that I could no longer admire him but must fear him.

When Klara left us, a term and a half later,
victim of a disease that was never named,
the school held a kind of service; a few of her friends,
the Principal and several teachers said some words,
and Mr Wilkinson's speech was by far the longest.
He was the only one who mentioned her city,
pronouncing it like a fifth-generation Pole.
But as I gazed from the front row into his features
there was that blankness again, the emptied eyes,
the lip held in a curl, a cheekbone glinting,
and the proud, once noble neck smooth and ambiguous …

But was it so?
For forty years I've wrestled with Mr Wilkinson,
trying to reiterate those mad, chilling seconds
when my callow imaginings welled up and descended
into nightmare. To no avail:
I cannot bring him back – except in dreams.
The first was soon after Klara: he stood there,

tall and protective, an atlas cradled to his barrel chest,
a razor-sharpened pencil in his hand, his features luminous
against the silhouette of a mysterious city.
The eyes were diamonds, but they glittered with tears,
and the mouth was twisted in a sneer of grief.
He reached out towards me
with the hand that held the pencil, and was gone.
I knew I'd meet him again, many times.

Elegy

Where, then, is the unravelled vortex,
the centre, the heart of that twirling in the great midday
windmill on a stick streaming its Saturns of colour
twisted into glossy loops and bows
and glistening in the steel-blue majesty of sky
on the promenade sloping up into the park we never abandon?

Does it ever really unravel, even after
we discover it dumped, a decade late, on a pile of dusty playthings
in a box up near the landing, the one
with the broken step and the protruding nail, where once
our favourite teddy came to grief and revealed all
the unsayable meanings of a word so precious and elusive?

So that when, one day, the once-shivering strips of celluloid
clasped together by a cunning pin and twisted
into the essence of childhood itself
hang brittle, faded and irreparable, the stud
long missing, the sun disentangled
above a gloomy wand half-cracked and warped;
when we uncover them one day next to the old blocks
and the red locomotive that meant all life to us –
then we must accept
that the windmill's heart is broken and beyond unravelling,
because it is time which has undone it
not *our* clumsy fingers on a bright promenade;
these would have yielded one mystery, yes, instantly,
but perished the other – like a balloon
pricked into its fatal confession,
when it is too late because it is death which has snatched
truth from its cladding and held it up and sneered:
'See! This is what you wanted,
this is what you were itching to know … Now
take it, it's yours, you've earned it!'

Thus the carton of toys, thus
yes, the helium of *desire*, or the lace-filigree of youth
too fragile and too limpid to be torn
until our timing then our curiosity grows tainted
with the sheer spell of knowing –
the fragrance of possession, the shudder of attaining
and reattaining eternally that which we refuse to consider
unknowable therefore unthinkable
and holy …

That which we must tarnish, over and over again,
desperate to encircle it through knowledge,
through one ultimate savouring that must resolve all questions
and put our spirit and our skin to rest –
for which we will forever rummage and jostle among the toys
allowed us, or forbidden, until
we discover them broken, barely known, unravelled at last.

The Violin-maker, the Forest and the Clock

I

    Into the thatched night
along the rickety wagon-rutted road
that curved beyond the village
with its fourteenth-century church
and its yard of graves and its cross
and the infinite well creaking
on its thick bucket like a bad G
(or the salty delicious hum of the sea
imagined by ages of children fresh
from fables and antique deceits told night
after night by twinkling old fathers
and aunts), reaching deep
into a difficult earth where water
and blood cleanse a geology
creased by the grating of the earth's teeth
against teeth and teeth against time
and the subterranean wind
washes the rock's knowledge and its dream …

    Beyond the chicken-scattered dusk
winding along the forest edge
like a farmyard ghost, into
the line of glittering firs
that escort the road, into the wood
darkening under its cool brood,
the irony of trunks that loom
to define and defend the roof of the day,
where footsteps lose themselves in
swift leaves, where sound tapers down
to the rustle of a faraway sun
somewhere above and beyond the trees,
down to the essence of sound, the beat

of the heart and the humming lilt
of the season's sap running deep
through the earth, the hypnotic trunks
reaching beyond thought, the clustered
guilts of mushrooms, cream and tawny and red,
sucking into the roots' slope
against the gathering trees ...

    Past tangled ferns and darked
clearings and slopes flooded with petals
of all imaginable hues, rushing
undulant into the distance of clocks,
swimming drunk among loops
of secluded streams, berry-provendered
apple and pumpkin and sunflower
resonant earths, and
creaking bridges and stiles a thousand
memories old, like the half-sunken machines
or rusting wheels of abandoned mines
and forgotten rail-ways scrubbed
into the pre-industrial earth, girders
and shafts and indecipherable parts
strewn in the jealous grass like thoughts
too difficult to bury or too strange,
and faint pathways etched only just
within the grasp of sight
uneasy and familiar as a dream
of destinations too dark to name ...

    And there it is. Call it a cottage
or a forest house leaning on its hip, thatched
to the hilt, the straw benign but holding up
a roof that would collapse if required
to account for itself, yet a too straight
peruke, like the dowdy concert-goers
at the Imperial Court longing to be crowned

in their dotage by the sprig of youth
but caring when all is said and nothing done
only for the music after all.

      Come closer. The walls must be of wood,
the chimney hints at smoke, the door, buried
amid a husk of ferns and flower-buckets,
ancient barrows and a box of rope, is
overarched with strays of willow-blossom
from the sobbing patrician trunk
that guards the gravelly yard, the sparrows
flecked with dust, and an abandoned wagon
bristling with broken hopes.

      Approach, push through the surprising door.
Enter a world.

    II

      In front of a bench he stands,
the century scrawled across his features.
The room is hung with shadows:
from every wall
at every height up into the ceiling
(thatched with a brown straw held back by beams
of rough timber knotted with dirty corks)
a forest of hushed, fantastic icons
maintain a watch: violins,
in every complexion a tree could imagine,
of gold, caramel, brown and red,
suspend the cottage, and of all magnitudes
from tenth to full, and violas too,
even a cello in its corner sulk –
and there are the bows to break up the design
like random bar-lines, and a committee
of music-stands by the shy chimney

next to the piano black with humility,
its lid ajar and its keys, from a distance,
a luminous strip of infinity and truth
simmering in the dusky room like heat.
And as the eyes slowly accustom themselves
and the ears tune in to the silence
and to the universe hung behind it
and as the fingers twitch and the tongue
        pauses for breath
and the entering air fetches the elegant resins
and the dizzy fragrance of wood, varnish, glue,
and the senses begin to construct their own instrument
and the room starts to rotate, ever so slowly,
and the eyes accustom themselves
and the man is speaking ...

      'The universe makes no sense without music.'

      He shuffles round the room, but *legato*,
adjusting the tilt of a bow, the bend of a scroll,
he flicks a speck of dust from a fingerboard,
blows at another, flourishes a thumb
to trace the curve of a thick configuration
of figures in the corner by the writing-desk,
jabs his spectacles up off the bridge
of his nose and double-stops at the stove
where a score unfolds
into a music-stand charged with patience,
selects a rich violin, fondly nestles it
into his shoulder and his chin. 'I shall play you
a new Romance by Beethoven, or perhaps
a waltz by Komdy or Lugubrianov:
                            see if you can tell.'

      The line is honey, the intonation –
almost the razor Viotti can wield

or the Concertmaster at the Court Opera –
brushes the room with ribbons of colour
that float to the floorboards, drift to the rafters
and shred the silence into fragments of thought
and shape into questions that can never be answered
but with questions that can never be answered.
His knuckles pulsate and his wrist is swimming
upstream through oil, down through geometry,
upward again. The chamber is turning.
                                          He laughs
up at the imaginary gods, he laughs
and lays down the music.

           Was it a minute, a week, an hour?
A pair of flames in twin candelabra
stands on the piano next to the chimney
and darkness is burning from outside the window
and time has visited
and something has happened
           but everything, nothing is altered.

           He shuffles, a secret smile in his beard,
the eyes are hillocked by the staved old brow
planted with tufts of occasional hair,
the bulbous nose will menace the lip
protruding moist and red and convivial,
the ears are missing, hidden abruptly
by a leathery cap that suddenly gleams
                                  on his skull;
and the spectacles glide to the bench
by the rocking-chair
next to a book bent to its aging,
its cover foxed and mottled with stains,
its blocking in ancient gold unreadable
in the dim room's darkening clutter,
in the violin room he is leaving.

III

Let us walk back now,
let us walk back to the city of time,
let us abandon the violin-maker
making his circuits around the cottage
clunking about with rods and buckets
collecting his daily chores.
We turn to regard him for one last moment,
the grasses lift to drown his figure,
he waves as if from another dimension,
a peculiar music is rising around us,
the cottage is sinking back in its valley,
we walk along a peculiar music,
walk back to the city of time.

Turn once again: all is now forest,
the house we visited never existed.
We plunge deep into the murmuring forest:
a sparrow forges a tall parabola,
a beam of daylight showers a clearing,
toadstools burn like huddling reflectors,
tree-trunks sway in their bleakest wisdom,
the wisdom of time, the wisdom of waiting
expecting nothing – a woodlark, a cuckoo,
a caterpillar hangs from a twitching leaf,
the pathway thickens, the clearings darken,
the leaves we are treading obey devoutly,
the forest darkens, we stop.

Somewhere beyond, a railroad glistens,
a mound that runs like an inverse river
from one horizon into another
across a green and yellowing century –
wheatfields, poppyfields, sunflowers sleeping,
the wading farmboys, the colourful women
in billowing skirts and ribbons that flutter

their Maypole colours for locomotives
that drag the city across these pastures,
whistle its warning and dwindle again.
And somewhere beyond, the farmhouses squatting,
their chimneys measuring out the minutes,
their breathing silent and safe.

    But we will not push beyond the forest,
the forest contains all we desire,
the city of time with its clocks and archways
can wait, continue, we are alone here:
we are alone with the murmuring forest –
we are complete, time is invisible.

    And now a question rises, hovers,
the creatures vanish as if to listen,
the branches pause, the trees inhale
a breath as deep as the endless forest,
the sky is a shimmer of leaves whispering –
an answer forms. Somewhere beyond,
an ancient artisan stops and chuckles.
You shoulder the fiddle and play.

from Vienna

I *Beethoven*

They say I was eccentric, or uncouth,
provincial, boisterous, or magnificent;
I shocked, or I inspired, destroyed, divined,
demolished, or appalled, or sanctified;
I prayed, or fulminated, I caressed, I sang,
they called me virtuoso, devil, conjuror;
I was the artist, the iconoclast, I wrecked,
or purified, was passion, pity, tenderness,
mercy and god – I was all of these things.

They say I bedazzled the unsuspecting
with music that could set their souls on fire,
some of them. Some of them slept,
and some kept whispering of war and money.
I wanted to shout with joy, defiance,
wanted to weep from the depth of melody,
release my spirit, pour out my testament …

War and money, and *love*, they whisper,
the city sleeps, drunkards in carriages;
I squint into the gutter, the parasol ladies
nod their indulgence in my direction,
their children point at the chubby stranger
with stick and trumpet passing the Schönbrunn,
or they avoid me, or they approach,
try to entrap me in conversation.

Drunkards in gutters, blood and money,
beggars spit at the passing carriages;
no more heroes – B. has betrayed me,
I have expunged him like a useless passage,
another erasure: we live and listen.

London's no better. The year I was born
an English sea-dog hit on a lump
of virgin earth in the southern oceans;
now that continent flows like a sewer
with all the offal of glorious Empire.

No more heroes, time will betray them,
time will avenge the glittering avenues.
Others will come to reclaim my music,
I shall inherit the generations
of saints and madmen – that's my despair
here in my rooms in the Schwarzspanierhaus.
At night when the silence grows even deeper
I watch the shadow-plays roam my ceiling,
I sense the footfall of ghosts and martyrs,
can taste the ashes. My city's future
whirls in my ear like a stormblown threnody,
the manuscript pages howl their fury,
the notes collide, the chords lie crumpled
and a pall descends on my shattered keyboard,
a hymn even I cannot hear …

Some nights, visions of hell accost me
(visions beyond what a mind can fathom):
I glimpse an age of unspeakable madness,
a time that will twist and disfigure my music –
I see it flow in the blood-drenched gutters,
I see it poured on the howling bonfires,
the notes exploding, the pages melting,
my manuscripts longing to burn …
I awake, unlatch the window, gaze
on a city in slumber, deaf and implacable.
I see you clearly, crystal Vienna,
and I can hear you, and I can hear you:
looming, eternal, and damned.

IV *Hitler*

Schicklgruber Schicklgruber
One day I'll show you Schicklgruber

The Donau flows, the Donau flows
Into the sea the Donau goes

The sea is black as the forest was black
The river flows and can never flow back

The forest swims on a sheet of white
The snow will melt in the black of night

The insects crawl but the birds arrive
The birds will swallow the worms alive

The eagle will shelter among the trees
His wings will open into the breeze

The wind will roar as the rivers blaze
The cities will utter a hymn of praise

The people will shout and mountains cower
The nations will know a People's power

A flood once carried the world away
I'll show you Schicklgruber one day

V *Schoenberg*

If times were different our music would be different.
I should put this city out of its misery,
abandon this continent – sail for Australia!
It seems I have repudiated gravity,
so why not plummet to the bottom of the world?
Or else I should wait for my Commendatore,
or my Virgil intoning mellifluous triads,
till the orchestra bellows its invitation
and I hurl my manuscripts into the hellfire
and leap in after them, leap in and follow them
down to where the Devil awaits with his tritones:
he who reputedly understands my music.

My music's not modern, it is just played badly.
The sound of a language must echo its morals,
what could the moralists have expected from me?
If our times were different music would be different:
this city is choking, the ghost of Beethoven
strides the battlements in disconsolate fury,
some nights he visits me – I awake trembling.
'You can never avenge me, you are not worthy,'
he hisses. 'They cannot hear you, abandon them
to their sweet reflections. The thing you are seeking
is not attainable, do you think they listened
when *I* was clamouring, why should they listen now?'

Maybe he's right – the tonescape trembles,
clouds over Europe grow monochromatic:
I need darker magic to conquer this mountain
than a pact with Darkness could bestow upon me.
The critics chortle under their spectacles,
friends evaporate, or the trenches took them.
And Mahler, the lion tormented, the painter
of spirit and matter – who never quite trusted
my new cosmography, yet one of the few

to *listen* ... Gone. How many summers ago?
Even Alban and Anton grow pale, mysterious,
distracted, like sons who must curtsy and scatter.

The scuttering clouds will enforce my decision,
the cripples are roaring, the clowns are a-tumbling,
the Austrian maestro knows well his orchestra.
There are times when I study my scored reflection,
scrape at the glass with my stubborn parchment
to discover, squinting, nodding hospitably,
my indulgent familiar, that wandering Jew ...
The bureaucrats stutter beneath their spectacles,
or they interrogate me – I awake trembling;
Vienna will find the Millennium without me,
the zodiac crumbles, the world is shrinking, sickens,
will suffer, the world will be ever the same.

After the Future

for Manfred Jurgensen

After the future, we abandoned
the eternity principle. Squinting,
we replaced the ochres and siennas,
the pastels of evening, with dawn's
dazzling hubris. The horizon
didn't move: still the horizon waited.
We stopped seeking after proof, content
to rest at last on the evidence.
Whenever we strolled the esplanades,
so proud in the merciless noon,
our sweat trickled onto our lips
but our voices never dropped
to a whisper, for we never mentioned
the times before the future,
never recalled the impossible, ours
was the esplanade in the merciless noon,
the dazzling hubris of dawn.

    The impossible was impossible.

We strolled the canyons
of our extraordinary cities, our words
hummed about our heads
like precision. The machines we built
crowded the circling horizon, which waited
in silhouette but withdrew astutely
whenever we neared the humming machines,
their perfect rhythm and pitch.
Sometimes, yes, we composed the impossible.
Away from the canyons, away from the esplanades,
concealed from the black impossible sky
with its morbid illusions of light,
we would scatter improbable chords in our sleep,

curling our fingers in meaningless litanies
that rhymed like nothing we ever remembered
in the dazzling hubris of dawn.
Our children would come to reclaim us loudly,
shake the dark from our sweating lips,
unfold their pictures of canyons and esplanades,
their eyes lighting the crowded horizons:
each like a lantern reflecting eternity,
each like a glittering dawn.

The Guilt Factory

From far away it is a constellation
of cubes and cylinders, pyramids and spheres
that interrupt the night-infested sky.
From closer up the shapes take substance,
and immensity, shadows expose texture,
structures reveal their form. But barely a sound
escapes the network of imposing designs:
platforms, barracks, engine-halls and towers,
and the myriad smaller annexes and links
that cluster the system – no sound, except
a faint monotonous hum, sometimes transmuted
to a rhythmic pulse as if from aeons away,
inferred only from the expectant air,
the haze shivering over certain canopies,
or the expression on a wall or brickline.
Nobody knows how far below the ground
the construction flows, how far into the sky
its elements incline – nobody has circled
the factory from without, it is too vast.
And no-one has ever returned from the bowels
of the enclosure. Those who have even touched
the walls or looked into the outer corridors
report familiar images: lanterns, picture-rails,
a complex of washrooms, dormitories, a huge
curved auditorium where curtains hang,
and many signs warning of great danger.
The engine-rooms and the assembly-lines
are only seldom glimpsed, and those who try
to look more closely come back with memories
so confounded, or in such forgetful calm,
that nothing can be gleaned. There is a point,
it seems, beyond which none can go –
those that defy it are never heard of again.
But on one aspect all are unanimous:

inside the plant, inside its very soul,
resides a silence, shrill and impassable,
a silence that accuses, and annihilates
with its ferocious gaze. And from within,
moving in a procession ghostly as life,
the manufactured shapes slide endlessly
along their endless tunnels, to emerge
no-one knows where. Sometimes a filmy smoke
is registered above a funnel or a tower.
Nobody has ever dared to capture it,
let alone to inhale its dark perfume.
They say it is the very smoke of death
and that the factory must disseminate it
through every inch of the metropolis;
and yet the substances burning underneath
remain obscure. There are those who say
that time is non-existent in the factory,
that space is an illusion, that no light
penetrates from below. This may be true.
But in the night, if one dares to approach
and enter the compound, and place a hand
upon a wall and stare into the stone –
at night the factory glows.

Turning the Tableland

'At length he by death is back gammoned.'
— *Annals Register*, 1793

Pretend I am
the flyer from the front
Richthofen's nemesis
grinding his Stimorol
in retirement, still
skirting the treetops with a
goggle-eyed squint
and a stiff salute,
plotting his next
conquest at the Opera.

And yes, pretend
the old order
never crashed in flames
into the wide-eyed meadows
of the nineteenth century;
that while the wry land
looked on, mottled
by the all-knowing star,
the procession of phantoms
never continued
plodding its infinite charade;
that if the abyss
yawned discreetly
into the dawn of each
fresh decade, it was out
of sheer tedium,
no longer the fierce dry
hunger of the newborn;
that the abyss and Nietzsche's
echo do not understand
one another.

Or pretend you are
dicing from a closed fist,
rattle of all possible
worlds, your wrist
elastic but the nervy glee
of a god in your eye
but a god
half in love and half
suicidal, half
hoping for that double 1
half for double 6
and the wild run back
across the isosceles landscape,
red, green, red, green,
the wild run home
and into the dimmer channels
beyond home, where
the quiet bone box
with its mutable numbers
squats unamazed, immutable,
on its Apollonian ridge,
and when you look back
at last from your
slotted grave, you glimpse
at last the
remarkable fields and the
pity of it all.

The flyer
never leaves the front,
he retires
into a den full
of drapes and rusty medals,
paid visits by virgin contraltos
or smooth-arsed
rookie scribblers

in his daydreams, and at night
cased softly
by selected ghosts
that omitted to eject
into the smoky
sudden chequerboard
targeting his flung silk,
as he swoons wild
out of flimsy steel and down
towards the green and red
fields, the mad tilt
of his future.

The Centuries

It is necessary to remind oneself
that the nineteenth century never really left us:
it has been here all along, biding its time –
like the fussy old colonel exhumed one graveyard night
who, barely have the encrusted nails been wrenched free,
pushes the lid up and bellows,
'About bloody time – thought you'd *never* get here!'

It's there, back of the musty wardrobe,
concealed behind a loose brick, in a mouldy pouch;
between the bones of a wall, on yellow newsprint
lining the floorboards to preserve the names of the dead
in the South African War; under the house
in a blackened strongbox packed with Victorian cards;
next to the ruby cufflinks in a crevice behind the chimney;
or in the attic – the mahogany dresser, the doll's house
decades empty, the chest of drawers with the huge metal key
misplaced since memory, jammed with maps and titles.

It is necessary to remember, too,
that the twenty-first century has been amongst us forever:
it squats alone, or winks from the electric arcade,
yells at the top of its voice from the wall of a tram,
gazes all night into its binary navel,
and of course (remembrance being what it is)
continues to mutter to itself
from railway cars, burnt books, smoky cathedrals,
gutters with stains ancient and black as blood.

On the Road to Hell

They looked at each other. 'See you when we're dead.'
'Or see you on the road to Hell,' he said.

We must have stopped ten thousand times
    along the way. Sometimes we'd pause
to acknowledge an acquaintance, though
    many were those we merely nodded at.
Sometimes it was just to squint into a window,
    though the shops were so numerous
it was hard to decide. Sometimes we stopped
    to swap news with strangers,
unsure, like ourselves, of what to expect
    and clearly lost, their gaze intent
on some difficult direction. Sometimes
    to consult the ancient maps,
dog-eared and fading in our busy pockets,
    whether the way had branched behind us
and it wasn't we who were lost and missing,
    for we feared that time was short.
Sometimes, discovering a shaded glen
    or sheltered promontory, a pause allowed us
to sate ourselves on our few provisions
    or pluck wild berries that sprang from stone
as we watched, or drench our thirst
    in purple rivulets, or crumple to lust
in a grove of poplars when the heat of journey
    exhausted us. Sometimes we lingered
to listen to things deep and unbearable
    which lifted within like a sullen music
that never could be recalled. Sometimes
    to stare at impossible contraptions
that drifted like dreams behind or above us
    and were gone, or at grand mirages

staged upon skyways or silhouette hills
    and looming like mythical temple battlements,
or spired utopias, or rainbow-shouldered
    spirals of chaos whirling heavily,
now close, now remote, dripping with meanings
    that silenced themselves the very moment
we thought we might understand. Sometimes
    we turned to review the distance,
recall the byways we had quietly chosen,
    though every time the horizon swivelled
we found ourselves in unknown territory, found
    we could recognize neither the past
nor the virtual ground we stood on. Sometimes
    we panicked and thought of weeping,
scrambled for mirrors to sharpen our features
    and always found them, brilliant, reachable;
but drunk with a sun we could not determine,
    the compact rectangles flashed and dazzled,
we ingested nothing but light. Sometimes
    it was the impulse to cleanse our bodies
which made us pull up at a locked laboratory,
    abandoned schoolyard or domed planetarium,
but just as the gates seemed ready to open
    delay seemed foolish, we had to continue,
something was beckoning up ahead.
    Sometimes, rushing to save momentum,
we tripped on boulders and our good intentions
    to note a landmark before we forgot it
were constantly thwarted by thorns and obstacles
    out of nowhere. Sometimes it chanced
that we looked at each other, smiled severely
    or shrugged our bafflement, the gesture
imperfect as consolation and quickly squandered
    like breath escaping; so we proceeded,
for there was nothing but to continue,

    and all we could do was gaze at the mountains
bringing the distance closer and closer
    as they diminished, so we trudged towards them.
And except for this, and the flawless vision
    of colours clearing and colours darkening,
we would surely have gone insane.

The Man and the Map

The dead flags
Of a city square clattered
Their stone curse,

Moss climbed, paper
Cups swirled, yet on this
Thursday the sharp hour,

The mad whip
Across a spiteful bare
Dawn disturbed him

Not at all. Stood there
Studying the grim
Map of a great town spread

Arm to arm, now buckling
Now flapped badly
At middle crease, flimsy

As the sky … Glad
To have spotted him, strangely
A consolation against

The encroached week
And the Cathedral bells,
I was transfixed

By a man who wrestles
A map, who carries a shaggy
Coat, shabbily the hairs

Of his ankle glint, a shade
His chin and the eyes
Fish-mouths. Wednesday's faded

Print wearily tumbles
Across his boot, unstrung
And still. He turns

Away into the cluttered sun
But the sky shakes
Its head. He shakes first one

Then another face,
But nods into his map
Shivering with half a heart

Under a larrikin breeze. I scan
The ghosts
Aboard my singleminded tram

As it abandons him. The last
Frame is a man
Statued alone with a chart

Dying on his hands,
Nodding to the compass-points
For confirm, a bent

Smile staining his face –
Then, like a prophet
On a swirling precipice,

He lifts his arms aloft
To liberate the map …
It gathered stock, it almost

Hovered back to the earth
It mocked, before
The final gust grabbed

The limp sail of its cloth,
Levitated it
Like a triumphant glowing

Rug into the minarets.
He examined this, then sagged
As it disappeared

Behind a stone façade,
And crumpled to a knee; immersed
In a howl I still can see.

Palace Coup

Trying to look A rather than B mused,
the old low-tech Tycoon prepares
for his last trip over the shaky board
(and that forever squeaking plank
of company policy the slick six detest)
– a high-noon stampede, loosed basely
by these plugged-in prac-joking prols
who want a levelled vote for all,
the Firm's great way be damned!
So now the nails are exposed.
The Tycoon (they say it to his face
only when they pretend they didn't know
he heard) dismantles,
derricks his coat upon the scary stand
next to the cactus. All that glitters
on his tie, his terrible knuckles
and his teeth is gold – they abhor
the way he flashes his bare bucks,
but his old man and his old man
before them (and so fourth) flaunted
the lot, there's a line to hold.
He nuzzles his lordosis
into the ergomaniacal seat he's had
imported up from Norway's north,
fiddles with the clutch
of vanilla folders randomed artfully
behind his bad back
before the meet. He eyes the art
ringing the ebony antique escritoire:
all those ancient urns – heaps
of crackpottery! As for the pic
of silly naked nymphs in a French wood –
Playboy anyday! But the wife. Well,

half a brass razoo's too much
far as he's concerned. She and her
Rennwah and *Fun Hoch*!
But to the point (midday). This mob
has gone to jelly and the job
becomes unstandable – where were you
when you needed me, you
lumps of pathetic clay? And now to be
undignified by such a puny gang:
the pits. He stops,
smiles goldenly, comes at the icy desk,
ashes the timber with his thumb.
The gold grin dies, he sniffs.
'This is *my* company,' the Tycoon says.
'I hereby dissolve the board!' He knows
he can't, like that, but he adores
reactions. Is not life
just one dirty big bluff? The gang gaze
into his eyes. 'Just kidding,' he sighs,
and sits to be crucified.

A Marriage

And almost every night at half past twelve
he would escape to Beethoven. Mystic
that he was, he'd systematically shelve
all he was wearing, even the chauvinistic

badge of the Patriotic Front, and play the Emperor
without any clothes. When he reached
the first-movement cadenza he would enter a
trance like that of a sunbaker beached

on some stretch of burning eternity,
his bulk impassive but his hands
dispensing the dizziest fire, yet the hermit he
essentially remained on those mile-empty sands

would assert itself as the Allegro abruptly ended
and his fingers stiffened, dropped
to a musicless disconsolateness and landed
in his melanoma lap. He stopped

in mid-pause to turn the page, perhaps decided
he was too cool to proceed, so he redonned
the discarded bits of attire, briefly confided
something to his cat, then telephoned

his wife waiting considerately in the next
room, knitting a vest. She would emerge
into the salon, trying to look no more perplexed
than usual, humming an ancient dirge.

The Ferris Wheel

'You know, it was the tallest, meanest Wheel
I ever saw, and I'd been around
the country fairs for yonks. The boats
swung on their axles creaking helplessly,
the occasional scream of glee or pubescent terror
curved into the gull-infested sky
as the Wheel rumbled about its grand spiral
like some rusty planet learning entropy.

'Each bucket could hold a single shaky couple,
or a sprawled yobbo in studs and bulging fancies
Levi'd to the hilt with slicked-black
Brylcreem locks or tousled about in creative grunge.
And every bucket was a different colour –
I don't know how they did it, but each buggy
could be identified by its unique shade.

'One day I came along at about three
and spotted this gluey twosome board the Purple
and cruise up into the August air,
two lovebirds on a spirit-level perch.
I don't know why, but I watched them dreamily
as the orbiter picked up speed and they ascended,
and climbed oblivious into the top of their arc,
and then …
        it *stopped* – first time I'd seen it happen:
the Wheel came to a standstill, just as they
reached the zenith, necking and fondling each other.

'It took a couple of minutes before they noticed
something was slightly amiss – a crowd had gathered,
and as it happened these two were the only clients

on that particular spin of the Solarion
(that was the name of the Wheel) — all by themselves
a mile above the showgrounds, a breeze freshening,
his hand up her skirt or down her blouse,
her hand — but sudden as sunrise
it registered: they disentangled sheepishly,
and craned very slow and very rigid
over the edge of their seat. A mile below,
the ground was at the end of another world
which it now dawned upon them had receded
completely beyond their own — you get this panic
sometimes, when sudden jeopardy
or a nightmare's map drags you toward the precipice
and you're ready to promise anything, renounce, reform,
if only you'll manage to get out of this alive …
Well, I can only guess
what guilt or desperate impulse
on the part of this pair of fliers into the sun
may have contributed to what happened next.

                'Almost as one
they started to swing their platform,
slowly at first, careful not to disturb
the precious balance, but gaining confidence
and vigour as the sea-wind roughened. The noise
of that gross contraption! — suffering in all its joints
and making the Wheel tremble and strangely shiver,
while the crowd of upturned faces poured disbelief
into a sky gravid with some mute imminence
that didn't bear thinking about
but pressed its lurid compulsion
like the spell of a Blondin inching across his Niagara,
or the stunt pilot banking to tempt the impossible
(and we know, we simply know, the flame
or fireball and the oiled smoke that must follow).

'And so the chair, marooned, echoing steel
turning in steel, rocking and reeling madly
as if to parody the structure that sustained it,
inflated its arc, gyrating ever faster
until the afternoon itself began to shudder
and the whole universe was focused momentarily
upon a crazy couple in a mad basket
that spun the world and time around its axis.

'It swung at the top of that tower, inching up
toward some ultimate perpendicular nirvana,
lurching back from tangent to wild tangent
as the Wheel stood perplexed and paralysed –
I swear I thought the car must surely go
right over the top, and the thing would topple over,
when, out of that blue, a scream
                              re-emptied the silence:
a shriek of triumph, a howl of ecstasy
uttered in unison – and then I noticed
for the first time that they were holding each other
as if in a death-embrace, huddled, entwined
body to body on a space an epoch above us,
their knuckles and necks locked, a clasping bundle,
that now, slowly, started to ooze apart,
as the gondola shallowed into an afterglow.
And all at once there were two of them again,
a boy and a girl, I guess, sitting correctly.

'Had gravity been defied, deflated, spared?
mercy invoked? – the Wheel had stood its ground,
the little slab of peeling purple metal
on which the solar system had just been turning
had made its point, or had it? I'd give
the world to have drifted right up there with them –
not out of any lewd necessity

to trespass on their private exaltation,
but for the sheer perfect knowledge of that moment
when the Wheel caused something to stand still
that could be labelled time,
but was more than time
and less than time – no, for the sheer knowledge
of what it means to vanish. Yet I know
I'd never have dared to forget the fear of vanishing,
for I was alone
and all of my recklessness foolish against this one,
all of my petty braveries
the frenzy of a dreamer who must dream earth,
because the sky is too tall and dazzling …

'And as the cabin steadied and came to a stop
I heard the great machine utter a sigh,
metallic, like a melody almost human;
and with a last hollow shudder of resignation
it eased the box out of its frozen apogee
and began to float it quietly to earth.'

Some Precepts of Postmodern Mourning

There must be a body, but there needn't be.
The body must be remembered with some fondness:
there must be at least two eulogists, and a third
must have been detained by traffic or a death
and the service must proceed. Sex
must be mentioned, but preferably not, except at the wake
or the seance when most words are permissible again.
On second thought, this precept needn't apply.
But at least one text must be read from,
preferably composed by the body and significant; it
must include expletives, but needn't do so.
Everyone must look dignified and important, or at least
significant; move deliberately but not heavily; smile
but laugh once only. Black must be avoided,
except in socks and sunglasses, which must be worn
during the service as well as outside afterwards.
There must at least be a reference to Celtic poetry
or Jewish ancestry, and both Testaments must be drawn upon.
Someone must remark 'I still can't believe it'
then 'Yes I can', and someone must respond
with a philosophical but solicitous lift of an eyebrow.
One of the mourners must be overheard to whisper,
'I'm surprised she didn't come, though it doesn't
surprise me.' It must be noted that the body
could never suffer fools gladly, and someone
must observe how much he or she is only now learning
about the body. Someone must say at least one Italian thing
either to the mourners or to the body, but a French
or German or Latin or Spanish or Sanskrit thing
will do, or a thing in any other accredited language,
provided the expression is significant. There must be
no public mysticism, though there may be, and coffee
or white wine must be served afterwards. Someone

needs to be squinting tears, preferably a large man
in a double-breasted suit with a crimson kerchief
protruding rudely, coupled with a pallid pusillanimous
niece with a weak chin and beatific smile
nodding with significance. Reincarnation must be accepted
by at least half the mourners, but not mentioned,
though strange omens and premonitions over recent weeks
must be seen as significant in retrospect.
The body must be understood to be pleased with the service,
the simple dignity and grace of the occasion,
the Baroque cantata, the words, the weather. Everything
must be just so. Everything must be significant.
Though in the end it needn't be. Later, this in itself
must be acknowledged as most significant of all,
or at least put down to the quintessential irony of death.

Supper Song

The perfect utterance is not enough
The measured utterance The disembodied face
Baying at the moon
Is not enough You are not
And I am not enough To have been guided
Out of Egypt is not enough
Climbed to the pinnacle
Of ashes or the point of a pin is not enough
To have danced in the storm Danced
Inside the needle's eye Danced upon the tongue
Of a fat flame is not enough
To have stared stared into the eye
Of the needle or curled into its thin comfort
Is not enough The comfort
Of blistering flame The slash
Of blistering ice in the jaws of dawn
Is not enough The knife
Turning gold in its glistening hand
Is not enough And the flung stone And the lamp
At midnight
Sweating a thin song is not enough
                                      No song
Is enough without the inconsolable tide No word
Enough without the groan under the earth
The dizzy sudden shock of a plummeting flight
Downward into the well of a dream
Down into the square cell
At the staircase foot No fever No magical flute
Is enough without the shuddering breath
No lie enough without its drunken truth
No life without its death O pathos
Of the spheres

Dreams of Dead Poets

Time was, I would have died for such adulation,
    given up a decade for a day of it.
My volumes dance in all the literate bookshops,
    pupils sift my enjambments for a sign,
my symbols scatter like dust about the land
    and all the quarterly reviewers now
drop my old name as if it were a chant.
    In short, I am a poet on the crest of fame
every anthology's incomplete without,
    my statue looms erect in pantheons
and I've inspired a thousand lesser gods.

Yet as I sit and scan the other side
    a horrible despair encircles me.
I've learnt about the suffering of the dead –
    much blacker than the half-blind pangs of life.
I am objective, but not yet detached
    enough from that poor ego I inhabited
to stay unmoved by seeing what I see.
    The stuff's no good!
The lines I sweated over mock me now;
    those random clusters of inspired gloss
stand like a sentence, and my cleverness,
    that self-reflecting eloquent façade,
haunts immortality from the halls of time.
    I can see through it all –
I was no poet: yet I could have been,
    perhaps, perhaps, if I had stopped to hear
that which was truly happening within.
    And oh, the verses I could *now* create
from these half-listened-to, half-done designs!
    I could rewrite my whole inheritance –
or most of it: there is the poem or two …

I curse this clarity!
    Soon it may scarcely matter. But now I'm helled,
like a poet at night, in one last desperate quest:
    I must find Milton, Botticelli, Bach.
There are some urgent things I need to know.

from *Autographs*

(2008)

Possession

THE BOY catches sight of the blue balloon. He is standing in the courtyard of a museum. He watches the girl who possesses the balloon. She bounces it along the asphalt, rolls it on the grass, bumps it into the air. The blue balloon fills the sky as it rises and dips. The boy is mesmerized by the balloon, he would like to possess one just like it. He knows he cannot approach the girl and take the balloon from her (he is too gentle), or ask to borrow it (he is too shy), but from that moment he can think of nothing but the blue balloon. He returns inside the museum, circles the exhibits: antique toys and artefacts, illuminated manuscripts, quaint instruments of music, replicas of weapons, photographs of notorious battles, a model torture-chamber, an ancient sarcophagus with its lid ajar. He studies these things with cursory interest; for his mind keeps returning to the blue balloon. He sits on a bench, pulls a pencil and pad from his satchel, tries to draw the balloon, with and without the girl. He cannot quite capture the balloon's elusive perfection, and he cannot quite remember her face. Suddenly the girl is alongside him, peering into the casket with the slanting lid. She cradles the blue balloon behind her. The boy could almost reach out and touch it, she wouldn't even notice. But this could spoil his delicious dream of the balloon, already swirling breathless in his imaginings, awaiting sleep.

Supplication

LET THE FILM turn before it touches the Moment. Let the motorcade stop, drift backward down the plaza. Let the jetliner freeze, metres short of the tower, flow back out of the frame like a toy wing at the sling's limit. Let the black plumes billowing from the edifice be reinhaled to unmask the blue. Let the bullet thread with a thud back in the barrel crouching in the gateway, the victim clinch his scarf and vanish within. Let the high sniper crawl from his perch, crabble back down the fire-escape, the drunken messenger lift his stone boot from the pedal, his machine veer backward from the X. Let the siren's wail diminish again, let the smoke be sucked back, the ovens clang open. Let the battalions pause on their relentless march, the battleships heave about, the bombs plunge upward. Let the tanks unroll, let the stormtroops halt, pummel grotesquely backward down the boulevard, let the proud man-children in camouflage watch their rifles fetched from their palms, the proud inflamed barefoot boy-children receive their stones flung back in their fists. Let fists unfurl. Let hearts. Let every prayer open with *Amen*, each breath be the ending of a prayer without words. Let words unravel, and all manner of thoughts, and things done and undone, let the Moment be immaculate and true, untouchable as a dream. And let the days unfold and fold back again, so that as we awaken and begin to forget the dream, we remember the Moment.

Mirror

EACH SOUL is the hostage of its own deeds, says the Koran. The city breathes in time with the music of myriad souls. They flock to the amphitheatres, they scatter from the rain when it lashes the metropolis, assemble in shops and street-palaces, repose in livingrooms observing their parcels of dreams. The clock grows dizzy, the season declines. Each day they collect their ransoms, paid by themselves into their private books. The scroll grows thick as it unwinds. It would be impossible to compute the sum, on a single day, of all the thoughts and deeds transacted in the city. An endless book, is the city of myriad souls – it would be necessary at once to read each letter of every word on all the pages of this endless book in order truly to understand the city. Perhaps only children understand the city – they cradle their colourful balloons past windowfronts full of words and inventions; they run along alleyways blind to the glistening sky. They do not require anything of the sky – the sky, they understand, will always open above, but the city will vanish the moment they close their eyes. They will be given lullabies, they will unwrap their parcels of dreams, their breath will trace an unransomed sleep to the music of an endless book. Meanwhile, as the amphitheatres and palaces grow dim, the rain will return – and who, then, among the city's myriad weeping souls will not envision tranquil gardens watered by running streams?

Amphora

HE CRADLES between his palms a time-traveller from the seventh century. A slender ceramic jar with twin handles, pert as a young girl akimbo. It is adorned with the most exquisite designs, dancers who could almost be Grecian but come (he's been told) from Araby. He shivers at the thought of what he is holding. Fourteen hundred years, more or less: the six-hundreds. A century like any other? More or less. From Great Gregory's twilight and the first churchbell in Rome, to Wang Wei and the last death of Carthage. In between, the relentless tapestry – stones climbing and rocks crumbling, seasons rotating, the birth of new faiths. How faithfully time fills its vessels. And now, with what shaky faith his fingers enfold this one. He focuses on the silhouettes curving under his care, these demigods or mortals, and remembers Keats. Abruptly he is overwhelmed by the fragility – of time, the unheard melodies, everything. The precious urn glistens with refracted light. He glances outward through the clever, gently tinted hollow in the wall, down onto the great city, its prolific rivers, the smoky despondent haze airbrushed about the horizon like some retoucher's reply. The lobby lifts continue their piston sarabande, the earth tingles in his hands. Just how long *shall* it remain, he asks the poet. Reckons the distance from his knuckles to the concrete floor is half a second – or eternity. His wrist trembles, the sky glimmers with thunder. He tarries, lets the thought drop.

Bite

THEY ENTER two by two, abandon twilight to its own defence. The clouds have blackened, burst their moorings, it's pounding animals of every kind, the gutters teem, the downpipes profusely bleed, the noise, the noise. All eight secure, I speculate refreshments, they concede. A lemon squash, a diet Coke, a double malt, a double malt, brandy with ice, vodka, pineapple juice. I swivel the third Glenlivet for myself. The nibbles come: bruschetta, vegetable rolls, we dissect the elapsed elections. The weather roars, the staircase clatters and clumps, our two housemates dismount, they're off to respective gigs but join the cabal *pro tem*. A cunning mobile bleeps, the daughter performs a stand. The son also rises, they vanish down the corridor, into the downpour's decibel gloom. Front exit bangs. We trickle to the dining-room, I allocate portfolios, we sit to deliberate. Entrée concerns the unravelling Atlantic pact, over a cylinder of herbal bread fuelled with zucchini soup. I uncork a debatable shiraz while cannelloni's dealt, followed by a discourse on the discord in the D of C, a heaped salad in Greek, immense potato latkes, a thing the PM said. The French come in for a serve, lightning attends, it's very pouring still. One diner, swept up in the drink, is filibustering on the Middle East, rapidly losing votes; his better quarter delivers a west-bank jab, he sinks like a fiery moon. The rain apart, the new silence is singed. Sorbet, coffee soon. I flaunt my cleanskin to tender a burnt toast.

Ladies

TWO LADIES taking tea across a coffee slab. One lady pours, other lady pouts, they are spatting, it would seem, doubtless upon a trite demeanour by one miss or the next. One wonders what. The other likewise wonders, her gaze wanders to the scotchfinger tray, her left arm lifts, her left hand hands the tray, a gesture of conciliation you could say. One lady declines with a churlish declination of the nose, the brows, the barometer hums. One lady sniffs, sidles away with her eye, other lady snuffles at her specs, strains to wipe a speck ostensibly spoiling her lens. One lady relents, reclines to take the cake. Other lady fumbles for a flask, flicks a finger of scotch into her crystal cup, a nip cup neatly rimmed with crimson from a lip, likes a nip after a nap, and a shot can fix a spat. One lady nods, other deposits an extra trickle, blinks, admires again the golden glow the paisley curtains cannot close, the gold at the rainbow's end, the tiny cup succeeding where the mug left off. Other lady opines on the colour in common between the day's ambrosial brews, the cool amber pond with its ferocious friendly fumes, the hot ambery well laced with a lemon moon. One lady grins, rattling her gums, other lady laughs, or rather chortles under a chin, it would seem the little affray is done. Two ladies simultaneously crane for their canes, for a stroll in the setting sun.

Dance

AH, TREE ... Street afternoon quivers on tentacles of light, conjures the glimmer of a thing suddenly *strange*. Drop a thought-shutter, *keep* it strange, so the mere moment can sing. Cleanse memory of all meanings of tree. Envision; apperceive. How it could shock an otherworldly guest attuned to stern geometry! How it might prod the subearthen twistings of some floundering guilt! How it offers too this joyance of repose, tree-truth, those slantings of smoky textured light. Now say again – *meanings* of tree. Go on. Say treescape, skytree, canopy. The skull's labyrinths, the blood's arterial metropolis. Sapchart, ancestor-tree, the sempiternal seed – all the treeness of things, their treedom. Now reconstruct the first *touch* of tree: a trunk that frayed, bark that bled, a branch that broke. Ruckus of the excoriated stick rattling on fencerails as it ran, scrapings of the sharpended stick repatterning wetsand as it walked. Recall stick-talisman, stickwhip, swordstick – see stick-in-the-mud to hang a hat, stake-in-the-grass to block a spot, wandstick to strike a spell, canestick to cross a rickety bridge. *Let* the shutter stick. Ah yes, all those slantings of treelight, a scrawled in cement figure-eight, a stickfigure house, home, family, tree. Go back, down on one knee – assemble an album of collected leaves, each one a map, a season's colourchart. Pencil a forest-map with winding ways, a treehouse, childhood's mysterious chance – how long upon memory has it stood? Become lost again in that otherworld, paperworld, that 100 Aker Wood. Look. Stretch two arms into the sky, and dance.

Mood

DO YOU REMEMBER how I depicted somewhere, once, the sundayness of an afternoon going down in dust, ochre, beyond streets that smoked quietly in their knowledge? It was long ago. I was trying to capture a mood, a *memento mori*, that had haunted me (is that too strong a word?) ever since I could recall. Not constantly, just now and then, which made it all the keener – a sharp yet a dulling sensation, a kind of melancholy of the fading light. Maybe what Lowell called 'the doldrums of the sunset hour'? I should confess, the linkage does keep playing on my mind, because I've been preoccupied of late (I think I've told you this) with how alike we are, the lot of us. You know it was mostly with a salty grace that I once watched our comrades, so in love with future, sprinkle the starry talc of brotherhood about – though *I* desired no less! No, there *is* nothing new. They, and the thousand generations (bless them), taper down through time to some mythic dot of the first primeval *yes*, keep vigil under a sky that never managed to dissuade them – except, perhaps, at Vespers on a Sunday, when that sudden dusty, ochre vanity would darken their capes like a spreading stain. So we deafen ourselves, do we not, to that descending *no*, as we cross oceans under a moonless night that hums like silence within, clinging the while to our flimsy vessels under Melville's 'permitting stars'?

Home

THE LAST cluster of coins in his palm, the paper run done. Ten to seven, back to the paper shop, bicycle leaning around the back. Jump on, float freewheel down the hill on the battered bike, coat-tails flapping in the August breeze. He knows the streets, their islands of noise, their chequerboard smells, the smoke from kitchens and glum chimneys, the rattle and scrape of bacon frying, the hooting of ready kettles. He cuts a line along ramshackle laneways littered with bins and fallen palings, he carves a loop past the war memorial, the park, the terraces pigeoned with time. Overalled workers are slipping from doorways, cupping their matches, jingling their pockets, mothers in rollers are sweeping their doorsteps, the nightgowned toddlers dragging their blankets, their knuckles rubbing out dreams. He turns the corner, a cat is stretching the stain of sunshine that climbs the fence, and then the cottage, its door flung open, a lorry parked with its tailgate yawning. He cycles closer, stops by a lamp-post, watches a pair of burly carriers barging out from his door. Why are they taking the dressing-table, the radiogram, the refrigerator, the armchair that father used to snooze in, the wardrobe with all his toys? One by one the belongings are loaded into the van, he can't believe it. He inches forward, dodges a cupboard, slips inside where his mother is standing among the dwindled remains of a home. Her tearstained cheek rotates towards him, she smiles, nodding, just nodding.

Surrender

THE ADAGIO from Mahler's Tenth rises out of the deep, but she sees only Venice, the night sky trailing behind their *vaporetto* like a forgotten kite. Then the celebrated *piazzetta* gliding past, its millennial obelisk in Italy's colours a cubist flag, the infinite pigeons lifting, subsiding. In memory's film she is drifting over the bridges like a tourist now, their steps (together, alone) a cliché on the cobbles, the canals gleaming or surly, lascivious, truculent; resigned. She is forever returning to Venice, returning to reclaim herself – the prize she had fashioned out of such surrender, only to relinquish it to the currents that swept the long spine of Giudecca. But there can be no returning. Tonight, lost in the stalls of the auditorium, she feels all the faces of time upon her, whispering their curiosity and triumph. Mesmerized by the gondolier rowing so majestic from his podium, by his slow extrusions of a dream that refuses to fade, she shuts her eyes. In their little room near the old Jewish cemetery on the Lido, *he* had wept – while conducting the closing movement of the Fifth when they unearthed it, unbelievably, from the clock-radio's dusty static. He had dreamed of becoming a conductor, of bestriding some day Europe's colossal platforms; but the black waters that swallowed him knew better. Charon's striped henchmen, distraught enough, had circled the spot in vain, until next dawn. Then the homecoming, those decades of numbness. She still can't watch Visconti's *Adagietto* without weeping.

Encounters

THAT TIME, Turgenev said, when regrets are like hopes, and hopes like regrets, and youth has fled but old age not yet arrived. And meanings still evade us, perch behind the illusion on the glass, and reasons avoid us, and the face becomes the reason, the reason explained away. Some things are beyond explanation, it is all we can do to express them. Like the moment of recall from night, when we struggle to retrieve what it is we are trying to forget, to forget what we strain to remember. Reaching the provinces, how grand our relief to ascend to the windswept plateau beneath the ambiguous clouds, how fitting then to detest the printed ravines of the noisy lowland. But the city of memory looms behind sky's reflection – like a colossal craft that suddenly scrolls overhead, sliding a terrible magnificent ceiling across the mesa, its underside fabulous with eerie shapes and circuitries – to mock us with its infinite grandeur, or summon us on a journey of no return. But when we listen, the music is not alien; it knows us, inside-out. We hover then, we regret and hope, we struggle to find some kind of solid state between river and rock. When we look up again, the monolith has vanished. We scratch the sky for reasons, juggle meanings. So we worship it, maybe we call it God. Or take the middle path, as Montale said, between understanding nothing and too much; the province of the poet; of us all.

Village

TRUNDLE YOUR BICYCLE up from the tree-nestled immigrants' blocks, up onto the slender road, while feral kittens leap from rubbish-bins. Ride down into the village heart, past the cinema screening Cousteau's masks, where strips of discarded film lie about for small boys to skim. Wheel left into the main stretch, where the buses from Haifa stop, with snub noses, diesel perfume, lever-controlled doors. Past the hardware store with its gadgets, buckets and tools, the shopkeeper couple, your neighbours, whose bespectacled daughter is the friend who will forget you. Past the playground nook where you slipped between the spokes of a carousel, cracked your skull, cried bleeding all the way home. Out further, past the windows of the Hungarian dealer in stamps, his den, his paper jewels tweezered and sacred in his enlarging lens. Past the school where they gather on the grass for a class shot, where with tongues gliding they fashion a farewell booklet of colour-pencil sketches and messages for you. Out to your cousin's house, for laughter and Lego and a map of your new land, this splinter at the end of a long sea, and your first little English picture storybook, steam-shovel Steve, and at night a skyful of stars so low you could stumble, so dense that the heavens swirl. Back past the village shops again, the road to the cabins, the thousand cats, and that dark-haired girl you hugged in the sudden dusk, somehow never forgot.

Projections

WHAT IS IT about masks and capes, and midnight escapades, and the colour black? It's 1958 in a Rose Bay gloom (the Wintergarden, say): Wagner's overture engulfs the gritty screen, and the grim crusader, ensnared between those deathly spikes of steel, the walls still closing in from Saturday last, at last ingeniously escapes; 'The Batman!' screech the sprung crooks of 1943, the serial rolls. Shortly I'll be crouching over a pad to sketch that wondrous pointy slit-eyed cowl. Or 1960 at the Metro, Bondi Junction (facing the Coronet), where I rustle my ninepenny Smith's while my courage surges to Zorro's amazing sword ('the sign of justice done'); later I'll practise slashing an imaginary *Z*, will render on bluelined airmail sheets the mystique of his ebony blindfold, that spirit-level hat, the cheeky pencil moustache. And in between there's 1959, where *Sleeping Beauty* delivers a shriller charm: Maleficent is magnificent – for weeks I'll struggle at my miniature desk to never quite accomplish her bristling lines, her tempestuous cloak, the terrible horn-topped angular grandeur of her scowl … These (and others too) the instructors of a particular art: they empotion me, inflict the all-embracing myth, during that innocent universe where white is black. By 1977 the triggers of memory twitch when I countenance Vader's hollow metallic lament, his mantle all-enshrouding (night-mammal, blade-wizard, enchantress-witch), his helmet a masterstroke from the century's blackest hole. Let him keep. In a decade or two, a dark new hero will defy the screens of our sleep.

Room

THOSE MOMENTS when everything's all wrong. You confront the mirror, you drift round the room, unease, malaise, a kind of emptiness. It's in the stomach, in the throat, it's in the soul, wherever that may be. The room is square. The window and your desk look north across the street, where old George tosses objects from his window at the dogs, or neighbourgirls flit and flirt. The 1960s. The desk has books and pens, a greenish Remington or (sometimes) creamy National RQ-700 reel-to-reel, a wooden Staunton chessbox standing by, a metal desklamp, deeply red and leaning from the left. The western wall, where the oval mirror hangs, will show an American map (with a small Old Glory stuck on a stick) beside the Dreyer upright – polished, dark, with Thompson's *Little Fingers* (or some such) spread on the fold-down tab inside the lid – and a bookcase crammed with spines and diverse wondrous things. On the south a wardrobe, whose drawers conceal a childhood's treasury, from the little plastic jet a sudden Manila friend gave in farewell (at Hotel Avenue, where you ran the lifts) to games and tricks and hoarded keepsakes, and the marbles in those papery yellow tins from Quik. The east is bed, the one with curving silver bars at foot and head, where you cross countless nighttimes earplugged to your National 2-Band 8 (show-tunes, Davis Cup, Garner Ted). And from the middle, where the futility descends, you look west and reflect. You know some of the details are not quite correct.

Lustspiel

TIME LIES, but never mind. Bruckner's Fourth is spinning below the northern drapes, as I collect and recollect my oft-revisited twenties. A leathery two-tone EJ wagon, a slick yellow Datsun (its inscrutable rattle), the songs, the songs, the crosstown marathons! Or parked ambiguous on QE Drive, her eyes fuzzy with desire. All those missed rungs of passage. Would you call this nostalgia – or fantasy's tentacles? I'm trying to maintain decorum, hence this edgy obliqueness. Otherwise, I'd offer a plan of that little room under her mother's whitewashed residence, where we spend infinity never quite sharing our skin with one another; where we advance, retreat, frequently castle, until the party's adjourned; and years later the shocking resignation. Or, I could reawaken a second-floor flat closer to the bay, the stairs dizzy with certainty; and tapedecks, night-trains and docking manoeuvres, the abrupt silences of pleasure's mean rictus. Etcetera. Sure, I could play the sober inquisitor, recant the bending of magical spoons; but I would be untrue. For has anything altered? The eyes still shapen their gossamers of want, skin reconfigures the arches of desire, their unattainable trembling epiphanies. Maybe the mystery is answered by the stars: Zarathustra tasted the foreverness of things, and Bruckner (the Finale climaxing now) was propelled by faith. *Bewegt, doch nicht zu schnell.* Like the universe, the CD runs down. But music, like memory, hunger, stays slowly busy behind our quickenings. I reselect the first movement, lean back to revisit the past. Movingly, not too fast.

Radius

HE KNOWS it is all illusion, but is illusion not the true stuff of life? These glossy photos spread ringwise on the carpet, and he crosslegged at the spindle of the compass, circumscribing his implacable Camelot (his priceless belt of paper asteroids), pirouetting magnetic like Magic Robot on his round mirror to spin his pointer to the next Answer (a fresh one for every Question). He gathers up a print from '62: his dad in the brand-new station sedan parked in their Bondi drive. So vivid it could be now, or yesterday. Another afternoon: with his mum at sixteen in the Botanic Gardens, his shot of a meccano Opera House escalating just across the cove ... Stop! Change the subject. (Not these tones!) Why this constant hunt for the wisdom of the dead? He can wait. Let the gods have their film and fill of infinity. He is not about to donate an eye to drink with Mimir, he will drink alone, stumbling half-blind (granted) through this rocky kingdom, his sword too heavy, his shield too fine, but all his illusions intact. He scans the carpet, swivels, and stands for an instant high above history, raises his voice in sudden joy. (Joy, that spark of the gods!) He deserts his Stonehenge before the mood melts, makes for the park – where his adult daughter, his grown-up son, will never run little again! He sits on a bench and weeps for the dead past, for the sheer beauty of the world.

Dysphoria

CATCHING A TRAM, Kezelco ponders the hazards of daily living. This century's already looking a trifle shaky. The headlines, riddled with desperate puns, so bent on parading their tedious wit, are a symptom of the guilt, he speculates. The medium is smirking at the message; how modern. Yet the message terrifies. Kezelco still can see the unthinkable smoke pouring from Manhattan's twin totems, hear the roar of the Balinese inferno, touch the hot twisted steel of Madrid. Opening his broadsheet, he jostles a youngish neighbour, drops a *sorry*, the girl half-grunts, impaled on her lurid mag. He sinks into print: the mantras whisper through his fingers like a rosary: Kabul, Kashmir, Baghdad, Jerusalem, Gaza ... Elbow glued to his side, he flicks to the features. The editorial leads with asylum-seekers, follows with a tilt at the World Cup. A columnist chortles over traffic-jams and road-rage on the bridge. Another slams the onslaught of computer sex. A third embarks on date-rape, drug abuse. Kezelco skims the Letters chequerboard: today the closet-minded trump the unqualified, and one correspondent would abolish the mobile phone. Kezelco glares at the pedestrians marionetting past. There are things he will never understand – the economy, reality TV. He asks himself how safe he can really be, riding a tram through the heart of a bristling map. The surly maiden rears like a diver, rips at the cord. He returns to the nearest fold. A coloured diagram catches his eye. He studies a graph of the hole growing in the sky.

The

WE ARE the ones who watch, who notice all. We shelter in the furthest reaches of your sky, and in the deepest hidden spaces of your heart. You do not know us, yet we are as one with you. Those of you who reflect might call us God, though we are no such thing. Mostly you have no inkling we exist, yet you conduct your days mostly according to the guesses and the signs you sense from us, on the dim screens of your diurnal selves. And though you feel our presence sometimes, through the mist, or there behind the surface of your glass, you turn away. Alone at night you'll glimpse the shade of us, we are the indistinct companion in your dream, the voice you cannot place, the strange reply. We are the citizens of the town you conjure, the street you recognize, the dwelling part-familiar yet bizarre. We are the staircase you tumble down, the room pulsing with unremembered secrets, the wade in slowmotion down the endless hall. We are the longed-for land of might-have-been, impossible reunion, the place where every memory comes back to life. We are the sorcery you have hungered after, the intersection of the then and then. Yet we are *now*, there is no other time. We are the ones who watch, who notice all, who make all possible. Sometimes, caught unawares, a shiver passes and you pause, perplexed. Do not concern yourself. *We* understand who you are.

Haftarah

HOW BEAUTIFUL upon the mountains are the feet of the messenger of good tidings. Kezelco is profoundly stirred: he must remember this, reread *all* of Isaiah. The man to his left nudges a prayerbook, it thumps to the carpeted timber at his shiny shoes; the clumsy neighbour skews and squattles to collect, kisses the spine, returns the black volume to the ledge, tugs at his crinkled shawl. The pews are filling slowly, K. detects, turning a torn page. He skims the English gloss under the parallel text, scribbles a mental note to check 'theophany'. Back in uni days, downstairs in the oblong Library, a massive Webster stood open on its own pulpit. And ah, the euphoria down the broad steps at lunchtime to discover (say) 'cynosure'! – and he fresh from Copernicus, Kepler, Tycho Brahe, the stargazing they all studied. Up north the flames were flying, each campus shivered with megaphones and badges, the barricades went up. Kezelco rode the slow suburban buses to and fro. The swish of words on paper, the church silence of Stacks, a coffee-cup, a shallow cigarette; each nightsky full of new destinations, a future that never would set. He has framed those circumpolar days, they hang on the walls of his rickety soul, lit softly by the eye of time. The rabbi speaks. Laments the defeat of words, the hounds of war wagging their lurid tails. Kezelco stares at the spiky print, his eyelids droop, the two alphabets swirl. Each letter a messenger not announcing peace.

Mission

WHEN HE ARRIVED there was hardly anyone about. It was the dreary main street of a nondescript suburb within a city noted for its blandness. He took up a position in the civic square, began to speak, but the few passers-by who bothered to notice ignored the rantings of yet another zealot, so commonplace here of late. He needed a larger forum. At the intersection of Broadway and 42nd the throngs were endless, but oblivious. It was the same around Place de Gaulle, they spun by with barely a swivel. In the Plaza de Mayo there was no hope of attracting attention. Outside the Kremlin was gloom, a total absence of interest. On Tiananmen the police waved everyone on. In Trafalgar Square only the thin pigeons listened. At Bennelong Point the youngsters laughed and gestured. In New Delhi, Johannesburg, Jakarta, impossible to get a word in. He took stock. Maybe a more sharply targeted approach? But inside the Masjid al-Haram, around the Ka'aba, the crush of the faithful was deafening. In front of San Pietro they were all too preoccupied taking pictures. The Kotel, at the foot of the Temple Mount, was a wall of impenetrable supplicants. He was close to despair, or a demeanour to that effect. He ascended the great golden Dome, arms upraised in salutation, a thousand colours rainbowing the sky. His voice boomed out. The pilgrims, their eyes dazzled, scattered, afraid of a terrorist attack. Angry now, He decided on a small show of force.

Verberations

THERE ARE MANY sounds Kezelco can't abide. He makes a list, he adores making lists (lists are systems, systems are knowledge), lists that have interesting words. A list of unwelcome sounds? OK, let's see. He shudders at the thought of thumbnails scraping duco or scratching at a board (he could maybe condone chalk); detests the mindless arrogance of motorbikes that drown the sun (he likes it when they sputter gently, consequential); loathes the squeal of horrorstricken brakes pursued by that sickening thud (he'll exit to investigate); despises his neighbours when their DVD interrogates his study (he admires their cat); objects to progressions that end with an unresolved chord (he'll rush for a tonic like Bach); abhors a vacuum in conversation (but always favours the absence of needless noise); after a spell, he'll disrelish aloneness (solitude's different, he's been known to conduct solo chats); abominates bigots of any striation (compulsively unleashes *davka* the opposite line); he disdains with equal contempt hypocrisy and the one-eyed hack (racists, revisionists, cloudland deniers he consigns to a deadlier camp); condemns our indifference to the foreigner channels of pain (watches himself watching news on his plasma screen). So where does it end, begin? He doubles back. No list is ever complete, but there's something else: Kezelco *hates* the sound of two grown people exchanging insults in a sheltered space – both of them telling the truth, both of them wrong, each one a victim, each one deaf and blind. Laments the way it can muddle a child's mind.

Dialectic

SKIN TAKES OVER, the mind is mesmerized. Imagination leads, then follows. And all for what? How often he has pondered over that. What he wouldn't give to – get beneath, *inside*, explode the myth, interpret himself at last. Out on the city street, from a café stool, he watches the procession. Mesmerized. The carbon-copy girls saunter past, oblivious (K. reflects) to what they mean. Each one so different, each one so the same, each one a movement in a different key, on a scale built of endless microtones. Then he thinks of Zoë, her exotic alphabet, her exasperating four-letter smile. The way her voice can soothe him, mesmerize, a kind of ecstasy. *She's* oblivious too, or so she claims – that's Zoë all over for you (and for him!), forever denying herself like a nervous supplicant. Tonight he's in a hotel room, interstate, parading about naked before changing. The newsreader arrives – he almost turns his back to the pretty screen, to hide from her sudden gaze, then laughs out loud. He thinks of skin, fantasy's adoration, the great divide. (The forbidden Picture, the unspoken Word.) And all for what – those four or five throbs of joy. Eternal dialectic, each epoch mesmerized: Climax and Anticlimax, Come and Go. The currency super-inflated nowadays – every new page fleshed out, promises that cannot be escaped. Not that he really wants to. The glossy mag lies straddled across a chair, the shapes invigorate, the colours soothe. Like Zoë, whose voice he'll not hear again.

Conclave

YOUR GRAVITY too great to let light escape, you have rendered yourself invisible. There is no readable colour for the black hole in your heart. You, like the Moon, by darkness are uncannily become. When you materialize, (say) on Remembrance Day, a dove hangs from a silver chain around your neck, brought down by an expert bolt. It is the albatross of history, you bother half-reluctant to explain – then you negotiate eight centuries (say), to the eleventh month of 1215, the year of Runnymede, the day the third Pope Innocent, at the fourth Lateran, proclaimed the fifth Crusade, and there among his seventy decrees that grand epiphany: a patch of yellow cloth for Saracens and Jews, the model and the badge for every millenarian innocent thenceforth ... You see, I do understand. But, what takes place when you retire to your peculiar room, lean your relief against the double-deadlocked door, sliver the blinded window ten degrees, travel across the paper-minefield floor, fold into your documented desk and look about, the wallscape wall-to-wall with its forty cages of words, your wondrous ark of books? Do you ever (suddenly desperate) stand, and with one graceless abrogation of the hand skittle the desktop councillors of print like a wild loser at chess; and then, glaring into the blackness that descends, would you (almost) assail the books themselves, commit the ultimate sin? Or do you prime your pencil, pause, wipe your divided lens, and quietly commence to chart another patch of your soul?

Threshold

ONCE INSIDE the store, he examines many models before settling on the one he will take home. The salesperson endorses his choice – the best, most lifelike, nothing like those primitive blowup balloons. Ingenious features, ultra-realism, the latest software, beautifully turned. Just look at the face, so genuine – and you can regulate the expression (she demonstrates: the bland default demeanour morphs to a liquid smile). He pays in cash. Back home he draws the curtains, unwraps the solid cardboard casket, folds back the purple velvet, peers inside. He ponders the uncanny replicated girl. So *real* – almost *truer* than real! Carries her upstairs, lays her delicately on the eiderdown. The skin seems so *alive* – her flesh virtually glows, pulsates under his touch. He pulls back; scans the instructions in the operating manual, discovers wondrous secrets. Breasts subtly resizeable ('pert, pleasingly nippled'); eyes digitally tuned ('photoresponsive, with tracking focus'); the skin resilient ('firm but not unyielding'); limbs and joints fully flexible, the hands miraculous (fingers 'autonomous but utterly compliant'); buttocks immaculate ('warm, superbly furrowed'); the mouth a marvel (lips 'rich and creamy', tongue 'correctly moist'), programmable for gentle suction and/or sound. Finally, the mystic delta, shaded with silky down, and beneath – most dizzying of all – the padded cleft which, eased open discreetly, reveals a work of art: a simulacrum of the crossroads of desire down to the merest detail. He probes its intricacy, breathless with wanting. But he will be tender, he will take his time. Kezelco feels he can grow to love this woman.

Signs

HAVE YOU NOTICED how, when people say 'That's it, I'm *sure* it is', they really mean they're not? Kezelco has. He jots everything down. He has a fat aquamarine writer's block (calls it his 'nemo pad'), where he notates the duplicities of idiom like nobody's biz. A student of the dark side of the tongue, he relishes what's exotic, submundane – the slangs and arabesques of outrage, flattery's corkscrews, the savage breviary of the expostulant. He copperplates blue-notes overheard on trams, stalks playground perimeters for pimply jargot; he cruises lengthy bars, hopping from stool to stool for the glibbest cherrypepper plipped into a glass. In particular, he's kindled by the lexicographies of sex – its luscious tints, transliterations, its slips and solecisms, its fractal poetics. Kezelco has designed a typology (a chart of many columns, with headings such as Jocular, Vicious, Evasive, Impassioned, Plain) setting out the signs by which we nominate those things between our legs, and what they do. One day he'll make a book, a history and geography of That. But not just yet. For the present he's set himself a task. His dreams have been unsettling him of late, he wants to learn to travel the astral plane, to discover what they mean. Especially the one where he's facing a wall of words, while a virgin undresses behind him. (He's certain he wants to discover, but he isn't sure.) 'Have you noticed,' he questions a tipsy confidante, 'how what we dream of, we never *really* want?'

Shadow

THE KEEPER of the Registry of Dreams remembers nothing of his past. He can't recall the child he must have been, the boy who ran and shouted and threw stones, the youth who kissed his sweetheart in the rain, the lanky young apprentice conjuring files, the expert promoted to the tallest desk. He knows only the rhythms of his task, the day-and-nightly rubrics of the soul that he must catalogue and annotate, while his own history slumbers, lost among the long-forgotten archives of the self. And when *he* sleeps, his dreams are a single dream, it reappears the moment he shuts his eyes and lets the anthem of his weariness enfold him. It is a music woven seamlessly somewhere within that unremembered age; a dance of might-have-been; a stupendous fugue of the uncounted voices, the unnumbered worlds that populate his Registry. And it does its work. It nourishes the planet of his heart, corrects its orbit – so that when he wakes, he will want only to resume his craft, continue to retrieve and gloss and catalogue, tap with a soft proprietorial pride upon the console of his cluttered bench each time another absence is restored, an end resolved, a consequence attained. But there's one region of the night he'll never glimpse. The keeper of the Registry of Dreams will not recall the child *I* was, the little boy who ran, the youth who kissed, the paper conjurer destined to shadow him. That dream is mine alone.

Notes

Fugue
Zapruder: A dress manufacturer and camera enthusiast, Abraham Zapruder was taking a home movie of the Presidential motorcade as it moved past the Texas School Book Depository at 12.30 pm on 22 November 1963.

St Catherine: This monastery, at Mount Sinai, dates back to the 6th century and is dedicated to an Egyptian Christian martyred in Alexandria in the 4th century; her bones are preserved in a casket at the monastery. The church stands on the site of the Burning Bush, in which God appeared to Moses. Next to the church is a mosque built in the 11th century. A steep track leads to Mount Sinai, which the Arabs call Jabal Mussa (Mount of Moses).

Sleeve Notes
For my verse renditions of extracts from several of Mozart's letters of 1791 (sections III, IV, VI, VIII and XI) I drew upon, and am indebted to, two English editions of the correspondence: Hans Mersmann, *Letters of Wolfgang Amadeus Mozart*, translated by M. M. Bozman (Dover, 1972), and Emily Anderson, *The Letters of Mozart and His Family* (Macmillan, 1985).

The Date
Elias Canetti's statement may be found in his book of reflections, *The Human Province* (André Deutsch, 1985).

Bless Relaxes
Title and closure turn about a line from William Blake's 'Proverbs of Hell'.

Flash Pan
I am indebted to my late colleague and friend Jack Baldwin for the image of Marx condemned to an eternal game of Monopoly.

They Sing
Blechhammer and Peterswaldau were concentration camps. 'Pictures of Matchstick Men' (1968) was a hit song by the British rock band Status Quo.

Glissando
A *shtetl* (Yiddish for 'little town') is a Jewish town or village of the kind that once flourished through much of Eastern Europe, especially in Poland, Lithuania and Russia. Roman Vishniac's *A Vanished World* is one of a number of photographic essays in book form whose images movingly document Jewish life before the Holocaust.

Millennium
The reference is to *Chronicle of a Death Foretold* by Gabriel García Márquez (Picador, 1983); the closing line of the poem is a quotation from the novel.

Distorting Venice
Sirius 'was highly venerated by the ancient Egyptians, who regarded it as a token of the rising of the Nile and of a subsequent good harvest' (*Funk & Wagnalls New Encyclopedia*).

After Messiaen
The gesture is towards the *Quartet for the End of Time* by Olivier Messiaen, composed and first performed in a prisoner-of-war camp in Silesia in 1941.

Vienna
The 'B.' referred to by Beethoven is Napoleon. The Third Symphony was originally called 'Bonaparte' in honour of the great revolutionary hero. When Napoleon proclaimed himself Emperor in 1804, Beethoven was so enraged that he seized the score and tore up the title-page.

Schicklgruber: Hitler's father was illegitimate and for a time carried his mother's name, Schicklgruber. It was revived by Hitler's political opponents in Vienna in the 1930s.

Acknowledgments

Many of the poems that make up the opening section of new poems, *Towards the Equator*, have been published previously, some in slightly different form. Acknowledgment is gratefully made to the following journals, newspapers and anthologies:

Age, Australian Book Review, Australian Poetry Journal, Axon, Blast, Blue Dog, Canberra Times, Cordite, Das Gedicht (Germany), *Eureka Street, Five Poetry Journal, Island, Meanjin, Presence* (USA), *Salt, So Long Bulletin, Turnrow* (USA), *Weekend Australian, Wet Ink*; *Alhambra Poetry Calendar 2008: 366 classic and contemporary poems* (calendar and book, ed. Shafiq Naz, Alhambra, Belgium, 2008); *Australian Poetry since 1788* (ed. Geoffrey Lehmann and Robert Gray, UNSW Press, 2011); *Over There: Poems from Singapore and Australia* (ed. John Kinsella and Alvin Pang, Ethos Books, Singapore, 2008); *Poems in Perspex* (Max Harris Poetry Award 2007 anthology, ed. Ioana Petrescu, Cameron Fuller and Gill Ratcliff, Lythrum Press in association with Poetry and Poetics Centre, University of South Australia, 2008); *Poetry World: A collection of world poetry* (ed. Ashis Sanyal and Partha Raha, International Bengali Poetry Festival, Kolkata, India, 2012); *The Attitude of Cups: An anthology of Australian poetry about tea, wine and coffee* (ed. Sue Stanford, Melbourne Poets Union, 2011); *The Best Australian Poems 2003* (ed. Peter Craven), *2006* (ed. Dorothy Porter), *2007* (ed. Peter Rose), *2008* (ed. Peter Rose), and *2011* (ed. John Tranter), all published by Black Inc.; *The Best Australian Poetry 2003* (ed. Martin Duwell) and *2009* (ed. Alan Wearne), both published by University of Queensland Press; *The Penguin Anthology of Australian Poetry* (ed. John Kinsella, Penguin, 2009); *Voices Israel: Poetry from Israel & abroad* (ed. Johnmichael Simon, Voices Israel Group of Poets in English, Jerusalem, 2012).

'Boy' was shortlisted for the *Australian Book Review* Poetry Prize, 2006; 'Sanctum' won the *ABR* Poetry Prize, 2007; and 'Humility' was shortlisted for the Peter Porter Poetry Prize, 2011.

Three of the new poems also appeared in *The Attic*, a bilingual parallel-text edition of ten poems with French translations by Jacques Rancourt (ed. Elaine Lewis and Christine McKenzie, PEN Melbourne, 2013).

The five previous full-length collections represented in this book are:

The Rearrangement (1988, Melbourne University Press; 1996, Octave)
Sleeve Notes (1992, Hale & Iremonger, in association with Golvan Arts)
Infinite City: 100 Sonnetinas (1999, Five Islands Press; reprinted 2000)
The Man and the Map (2003, Five Islands Press)
Autographs: 56 poems in prose (2008, Hybrid Publishers)

All the poems contained in the first four books listed above can be accessed on the Australian Poetry Library website: http://www.poetrylibrary.edu.au/poets/skovron-alex.

***

I would like to thank the many friends, fellow-writers and editors – too many to mention individually – who have given me encouragement, advice and support over the past thirty-odd years. With regard to the present volume, I wish to express my especial gratitude to John Leonard and David Musgrave.

Alex Skovron is the author of five collections of poetry and a prose novella. His work has been published widely, and the numerous readings he has given include appearances in China, Serbia, India, Ireland, and on Norfolk Island. Among awards for his poetry are the Wesley Michel Wright Prize, the John Shaw Neilson Award, the *Australian Book Review* Poetry Prize, and for his first book, *The Rearrangement* (1988), the Anne Elder and Mary Gilmore awards. His novella, *The Poet*, was joint winner of the FAW Christina Stead Award for fiction, and has been translated into Czech. *The Attic*, a selection of his poetry with French translations, was published in 2013. Alex was born in Poland, lived briefly in Israel, and migrated to Australia in 1958, aged nearly ten. He is based in Melbourne and works as a freelance editor.

www.ingramcontent.com/pod-product-compliance
Lightning Source LLC
Chambersburg PA
CBHW011306150426
43191CB00017B/2355